Praise for
Sacred Sex

"*Sacred Sex* is a breath of fresh air that will help you and your mate recapture not only the excitement of sex but also the spiritual oneness God desires for you. We loved Tim's conversational and often humorous style and found the end-of-chapter questions to be great discussion starters."

—DAVID AND CLAUDIA ARP
founders of Marriage Alive seminars
and authors of *10 Great Dates*

"Tim Gardner's *Sacred Sex* is fresh, cleaver, grounded, and insightful. It's not simply a sex book for couples wanting to fire up passion in the bedroom, it is for all of us who are searching for the spiritual, even mystical, meaning of a husband and wife becoming one. Read this book, and your marriage—as well as your relationship with God—will never be the same."

—LES AND LESLIE PARROTT
Seattle Pacific University,
authors of *Saving Your Marriage Before It Starts*

"*Sacred Sex* is a must-read for many: The happily married will discover crucial information for being a better lover, the searching Christian will revel in the light that shines from a clear and practical theology, and the sexual struggler will learn from some great answers how to ask the right questions and make changes."

—DOUG ROSENAU
author of *A Celebration of Sex*
and professor at the Institute for Sexual Wholeness

"Can you say 'God, Jesus, and sex' together in one breath? *Sacred Sex* says yes and takes you into the secrets of holy sex."

—LINDA DILLOW AND LORRAINE PINTUS
coauthors of *Intimate Issues*

"Sacred sex isn't an oxymoron. Sacred sex isn't lukewarm sex. *Sacred Sex* will free many couples to begin to experience the joy and freedom of a fully spiritual and fully sexual relationship. Buy this book, read it, apply it, and with a smile on your face, you'll rediscover what it means to be fearfully and wonderfully made."

—GARY J. OLIVER, TH.M., PH.D.
executive director of the Center for Marriage and Family Studies
and professor of psychology and practical theology at John Brown University

"It's hard to imagine someone writing a book about sex so good that the book is more delightful than the subject matter. Actually, it's impossible. But Tim Gardner comes close. *Sacred Sex* is written with clarity, wit, and wisdom. May it find many readers."

—JOHN ORTBERG
teaching pastor at Willow Creek Community Church
and author of *If You Want to Walk on Water,
You've Got to Get Out of the Boat*

"I am impressed, really impressed by *Sacred Sex.* Dr. Gardner deals most insightfully with matters of ultimate intimacy yet never becomes vulgar or crudely sensual. This book should prove greatly helpful to couples, especially those who have conscientious scruples."

—DR. VERNON C. GROUNDS
chancellor of Denver Seminary

SACRED sex

a spiritual

celebration

of

oneness

in marriage

SACRED

sex

TIM ALAN GARDNER

foreword by Scott M. Stanley, Ph.D.

WATERBROOK
PRESS

SACRED SEX
PUBLISHED BY WATERBROOK PRESS
2375 Telstar Drive, Suite 160
Colorado Springs, Colorado 80920
A division of Random House, Inc.

Some of the stories in this book are composites of several different situations;
details and names have been changed to protect identities.

ISBN 0-7394-2697-4

Printed in the United States of America

To Amy:
My companion, advisor, teacher, encourager,
best friend, helpmeet, co-heir,
my lover and my wife with whom I am blessed to be one.
You bring out the best; you forgive the worst.
With all that I am and all that I'll ever be,
this book is wholly dedicated to you,
for without you, this book would never be.

Contents

Foreword

This is a book I've looked forward to for some time, and it was well worth the wait.

For years, I've been disturbed by the way Christians tend to think about marriage. We don't give enough thought to the implications of how God created us—as physical beings. The physical nature of our being should impact our thinking, our theology, and our models of marriage. And now, Tim Gardner helps us think through the implications.

With wonderful help and feedback from his wife, Amy, Tim goes where too few Christians have dared to go before. He takes us through a head-on look at the physical union between husband and wife and shows us how deeply embedded physical oneness is in God's design for marriage. The key point being this: Since God placed this physical union at the core of His teaching about oneness—by way of creation as well as revelation—then that deep truth should bear some imprint on how we live in marriage.

I first met Tim some years ago at a conference. We've talked many times since about marriage and especially about oneness in marriage. When we first began our discussions, I figured, "This guy sure likes to talk about sex!" In fact, he does. But there was something more than just a guy talking about sex. Here is a man who understands deep truths about oneness in marriage, and now he's sharing those truths with you.

I remember counseling a very wise couple many years ago who told me something I'd not heard before. They commented on the close connection between the sexual experience and Christian spirituality. This was something I'd never heard, yet I immediately knew it to be true. Deeply true. How had this truth escaped all the discussions and reading and writing about marriage that I've been immersed in for more than twenty years? A powerful observation was made by way of a simple statement: The sexual experience is closely tied to our experience of Christian spirituality.

Contrast that truth with the focus of much of the literature and talk about marriage in Christian circles. We often hear that there are a variety of ways couples can become one, and each of these ways needs to be nurtured and deepened in order for a couple to experience the fullest blessings in marriage. Many of us talk about oneness having four aspects: physical, emotional, intellectual, and spiritual. I agree that there is great value in pursuing oneness in each of these four areas. But we tend to neglect the first type of marital intimacy in our discussions. We touch briefly on physical intimacy, then quickly skip ahead to the latter three.

Further, and perhaps worse, we often talk about the latter three areas—emotional, intellectual, and spiritual—as the essential elements for creating the optimal conditions for physical intimacy. Rarely do we hear the reverse, that physical intimacy has the power to set the stage for the latter three. I'm not suggesting that couples can have great marriages simply by learning to have great sex. But it's clear that we've given far too little attention to something that's so obviously true and indicated all through Scripture: God placed the physical union between husband and wife at the very heart of marriage. When He introduced the first couple to the concept of oneness, physical union was the method He created to make it happen.

Tim takes this familiar but often misplaced truth and runs with it. So keep your eyes open and allow yourself to think deeply about what you've been told and what you know to be true. Think about the Bible's core teachings on oneness, starting with Adam and Eve. Like Tim, you might come to a rather important conclusion. God put this physical union thing right at the foundation of what oneness means in marriage. Among many other things, this means that sex for believers is not simply about drawing together in intense physical pleasure. There is nothing wrong with that, of course, when the pleasure is enjoyed within the commitment of marriage. But there is much more. In sex, there is the profound opportunity to explore and experience God's deepest truths about oneness, mystery, and love.

As the title of this book suggests, there is something sanctified about sex. It's clear that God set it apart and gave it great spiritual purpose. Do we live that way? Sadly, many who could embrace this truth don't. Tim's desire is to push your thinking about oneness in marriage. He's doing much more than simply helping Christian couples have better sex. He wants to help Christians get in touch with a rich theology of oneness that can lead to profound changes and depth of spiritual meaning in the physical union of husband and wife.

Nowhere in this book will you find pictures and diagrams or revolutionary new sexual techniques. Rather, you'll find a deeper vision of what oneness through sex is meant to be. May you be deeply blessed by God as you explore this profound aspect of His creation.

—SCOTT M. STANLEY, PH.D., coauthor of *A Lasting Promise*
and codirector of the Center for Marital and Family Studies
at the University of Denver

A Sacred Pleasure

Touching Souls Through Holy Sex

Holy sex? After reading two words, you may already think I'm off the deep end—really deep. How can I mention holiness and sex in the same phrase? Well, for one thing, because God does. While a lot of us have made a god out of sex, too few of us understand what God had in mind when He created sex. And while Christians acknowledge that God connects sex with oneness and reserves it for married couples only, most of us never experience the spiritual aspects of this sacred act.

Now, I don't pretend to have stumbled upon some secret truth that, until this point, has eluded the world's great minds. In light of that, why did I bother to write *another* book on s-e-x, a topic that has been written on more than the walls of the New York City subway system? It's a topic that fills a whole section at Barnes & Noble when, if I'd written on *The Art of Edsel Repair,* I could have had a section all to myself. Why write a book that will make my mother lament, "Where did I go wrong," make my church decide I should be on permanent sabbatical, and make my lovely wife strongly hint (kind of like the Godfather hints) that I should come up with a pen name, preferably one that begins with *Brother* and that would indicate I live in a Himalayan monastery? Why another book on sex? Because, as I read the current books on the topic (my wife will tell you I read way too many and should go back to Tom Clancy novels), I didn't find any that fully explore the deeper meaning of sex from God's perspective. There are shelves full of books that disclose more about sex than most of us care to know, but they fail to fully explain the one thing that makes sense of it all. And that one thing they miss is that sex is holy.

Sex doesn't make sense unless we understand that it is holy. We can't unlock the secrets of sex and enjoy its greatest benefits unless we approach it as a holy act. Only then will couples truly experience the beauty and joy of great sex the way God intended.

I'm a marital therapist and a pastor, a husband and a committed follower of Christ. In my work, I encounter people who are searching for answers to their sexual difficulties. Couples need to have a clear understanding of why God created sex, what He intended it to be, and how understanding these truths will move them to a place of joy, fulfillment, and even worship. No matter how much effort you put into it, sex will have no lasting, soul-touching meaning, and it won't be lived and enjoyed to the fullest, unless you understand the full purposes for which God created it. Thus, another book.

If you're looking for a new erogenous zone, a medical breakthrough for prolonging orgasm, or a way to have fabulous sex every time the notion crosses your mind, you have the wrong book. I do want people to experience exciting sex, but I don't believe that comes primarily through better technique or superior pharmaceuticals. However, if you're ready to begin a journey of sexual discovery that takes the focus off orgasm and puts it on oneness, you've come to the right place. If you're hungry for a fresh outlook that brings clarity and new wonder to the often-chaotic world of marital sex, then I invite you to join me on this journey.

The discovery of what God intends for sex and how He is involved in the sexual connection between spouses will permanently change a couple's life. And not just their sex life. Marital sex, when rightly understood and practiced, has benefits that spill over into the rest of a couple's relationship. Communication, intimacy, problem solving, teamwork, spiritual growth—every aspect of married life works better when a couple's sex life is practiced according to God's design. Learning the meaning of holy sex will give you not only a tremendous appreciation for sex and for each other, but most important, a new understanding of God's role in the experience of marital intimacy.

SEX AND THE MIND OF GOD

God, Jesus, and sex. These three words are seldom uttered in the same conversation. But they need to be not just with our spouses but also in our hearts and minds as we seek the optimum expression of our sexuality. As a counselor, I regularly see committed couples who love God and each other, but who wonder if sex is destroying their marriage. If God really did create sex and if He gave it to married couples as a singular gift just for us, why is sex such a struggle?

In trying to learn what actually happened with the first married couple in the Garden of Eden, I've read a multitude of books and talked with a number of professionals in the fields of counseling and theology. After all this study, years of talking and listening, and much prayer, I've put some ideas together about God, Jesus, and sex—three words that really do belong together. What I discovered was a revelation that changed not only my own life, but the lives of many couples I've taught and counseled.

It's important that we know that the Christian understanding of sexuality has gone through several shifts over the last fifteen hundred years. The first generation of thinking viewed sexuality simply as the required method of procreation, believing that God grudgingly tolerated the pleasurable part of the act because it motivated people to "be fruitful, and multiply" (Genesis 1:22, KJV). The second generation of thinking, coming centuries later, affirmed that God really does want us to enjoy sex. The pleasurable part is okay with Him. The third generation of thought, which surfaced only in the last quarter-century, popularized the notion that since God wants spouses to celebrate the pleasures of sex, we should take full advantage of the deluge of research and medical data that explains in great detail how it all works. According to this thinking, there was no longer any legitimate reason for Christians to put up with any sexual dysfunction. Instead, the time had come to not only embrace God's gift of sex, but also to take advantage of the technology that enhances its pleasure.

This evolution of Christian thinking in the area of sex is important, first to appreciate how the church has always seemed to struggle with an understanding of sex and, second, so we will learn that our current view of sex is not necessarily where God wants it to be. We need to celebrate the pleasure of marital sex, and it is helpful to understand the physiology and technique of this amazing act. But something big is still missing. Even with couples taking advantage of information, medication, and therapy that were unheard of a generation ago, overall sexual satisfaction remains frightfully low. But since we seem to have identified all of the pieces to the sexual puzzle, why do couples still report such widespread dissatisfaction? We'll explore the reasons in detail later, but that question does bring me to the fourth generation of Christian sexual understanding.

The latest development in Christian thinking regarding sex has to do with viewing it in the context of all of life, including our spiritual lives. It's time for Christian couples to enter the age of "meta-sex." (Sorry, guys, I didn't say *mega*.) Meta-sex goes beyond acknowledging that God intended sex to be a lot of fun. And it doesn't rely on learning all the correct techniques to make the big event even more exciting. Instead, meta-sex understands how everything *surrounding* the big event affects it in ways we don't expect. Meta-sex explores such questions as these: "What do I really believe about sex?" "How do the things I think and feel affect my sex life?" "What were God's original intentions when He created sex?" In sum, "Why sex?"

It is important to acknowledge that God could have arranged the whole reproduction thing any way He wanted: a hidden button, a super-secret handshake, or some unique facial exchange that brought about conception. Really, He could have. But instead, He designed sex. He must have had a good reason, but what is it? The answer, in short, is that God wanted sex to be a lot more than just a really fun thing for wives and husbands to do together. And He wanted it to be more than an extremely enjoyable way to populate the planet. He had a far loftier goal in mind. God designed marital sex to be an encounter with the divine. Sexual intimacy, with all of its overwhelming emotions and heart-pounding sensations, was never intended to be experienced solely in the emotional and physical realms. Rather, it is to be a spiritual, even mystical, experience in which two bodies become one. God is present in a very real way every time this happens.

Sex really is holy. It's a sacred place shared in the intimacy of marriage. And it's an act of worship, a sacrament of marriage that invites and welcomes the very presence of God. That's the meaning and benefit of holy sex.

In the following chapters, we'll avoid detailed discussions of technique and physiology and concentrate instead on the loving God who decided that since the creation of male and female, sex was to be the way that a husband and wife were to touch each other's soul. The essence of this book was part of my doctoral research project. A majority of the couples in the study group who processed and applied these principles registered statistically significant increases in their overall marital satisfaction as well as greater satisfaction with their expressions of affection. I can't promise the same results in every marriage. However, the data confirms that if we grow in our understanding of sex as a God-given, holy event, we will also grow in our satisfaction with our mates and with our marriages. I pray that this book will do just that for you.

May God bless you richly on this journey.

—TIM ALAN GARDNER, Westfield, Indiana, December 2001

Chapter 1

Holy Sex

What Makes This Human Act So Sacred?

> There may be some things better than sex, and
> there may be some things worse. But there's
> nothing exactly like it.
>
> —W. C. FIELDS

Sex is holy. It was created by God and given to His children to cherish and protect.

Sex is holy. This is why our world is so fascinated, so obsessed, and even so messed up about the subject of sex.

Sex is holy. That is why in my adolescent, premarital world of sexual musings and passions there were periods when I felt that everything about sex was created either to torment me or to leave me feeling guilty. And that is why, in the sanctity of my marriage, I've known times of sexual intimacy with my wife to be the very presence of God Himself.

Sex is holy. It can be, for those who are willing to enter this sacred space, a place of worship.[1]

I realize that it might seem ludicrous to equate sex with holiness and to describe it as an experience of truly worshiping God. How can something that has been so desecrated, so abused and polluted, and that has caused so much pain be considered a holy experience? And how, if we're talking about the adoration of the one true God, can the sexual act ever be considered an act of worship? How, with all its unseemly baggage, can sex be any of these things?

The full truth about sex is this: It is both sacred and polluted, holy and desecrated. The sacredness of sex is not based on how we treat it or mistreat it. Its sacredness is based on its essence, which comes from God. Sex is holy because God created it to be holy.

STANDING ON HOLY GROUND

The concept of holiness is at the heart of who God is, of what He calls His people to, and of what we encounter when we encounter Him. As Moses timidly approached a burning bush that wasn't consumed by the fire, he heard the One who had called him say, "Do not come any closer.... Take off your sandals, for the place where you are standing is holy ground" (Exodus 3:5). The Bible doesn't describe exactly what Moses did just then, but my bet is that he was barefoot before he could stammer "lowly sheepherder."

What made this scrap of desert especially holy? Two things. It was holy because the Holy One Himself was present there. But it was holy also because God had set that little piece of Mount Horeb apart for His use. The God of Abraham, Isaac, and Jacob, the same God who created the universe, had come to this desolate place to call His servant Moses and to set him apart to free God's people from slavery in Egypt. It was holy ground because of who was there and because of what He was doing there. God's presence and His purposes combined to transform an ordinary patch of desert into sacred space.

So what is it that makes sex, a desertlike patch of human experience for so many couples, a holy act? Two things. First, sex is holy because God

Himself is present whenever a wife and husband partake of His gift of sex. And second, sex is holy because the Creator of the universe designated the gift of sexual intimacy to be *the* way that a husband and a wife both create and re-create the God-designed oneness of marriage. Sex makes two people one because God declared it to be so. He has set apart sex for His use. It *is* holy ground.

THE MEANINGS OF HOLINESS

In the Scriptures, the word *holy* has several distinct meanings. First is the idea of something that is perfect, transcendent, and spiritually pure. The prophet Isaiah refers to God no less than twenty-five times as "the Holy One of Israel." It is Peter's description of Jesus when he proclaims: "We believe and know that you are the Holy One of God" (John 6:69).

Holiness also applies to things that God has designated as holy. In the Old Testament, the ark of the covenant was such an object. This fact is graphically illustrated in the story of Uzzah, a man who mistakenly believed his hand was somehow purer than the dirt[2] and was struck down by God for grabbing hold of the ark to keep it from touching the ground (2 Samuel 6:6-7).

The word *holy* is used to describe something that has been set apart by God and for God. Scholars refer to Leviticus 17–25 as the Holiness Code. This passage contains a myriad of commands, which the Hebrews were to obey so that they might be holy "because I, the LORD, am holy" (Leviticus 20:26). Places, priestly garments, items for worship, sacrificial animals, and the nation of Israel itself were all to be set apart for a special purpose—the purpose of honoring and glorifying the Most Holy God.

Finally, the word *holy* means to evoke adoration, worship, and even fear and trembling. It was our friend Peter's response when Jesus miraculously filled the boat with fish. Peter fell down at Jesus' knees, begging Him to depart because His holiness evoked Peter's sense of unworthiness (see Luke 5:8). This is no doubt how Moses felt when he lay prostrate and shoeless before God on the burning sand at Mount Horeb (see Exodus 3:5). The presence of the truly holy causes us to see our humanness and our own failures, and to pay humble homage to the only One who is sovereign and sacred.

Each of these four definitions of *holiness* applies to sex between a wife and a husband. First, sex is holy because it was created by the Holy One of Israel before sin ever entered the human race. In the beginning, sex was perfect and spiritually pure.

Sex is also holy because God designated it to be so, as we will understand more completely when we study the familiar story of the Garden of Eden. Like the ark of the covenant, which much later was regarded with awe and respect, the mystery of oneness that occurs between man and woman in the act of sex is to be accorded a similar holy and high regard. Although the ark is an object and sex is a relationship, both were designed by God; both are meant to be treated with the honor due that which is holy; and both are meant to be reminders of the One who is holy.

Further, sex is holy because God has set it apart from the dawn of time for His special purpose—the magnificent purpose of representing Christ and the church (see Ephesians 5:31-32). This was a mystery, hidden from humankind for ages, and revealed only after Christ ascended to the Father.

Finally, sex is holy because it can usher us into a genuine experience of worship. Just as the appearance of the burning bush filled Moses with awe, the true experience of oneness that God designed marital sex to be can bring us to a place of heartfelt praise and adoration of Him. It can leave us trembling at the wonder and beauty and love of almighty God, who gave us this incredible gift.

To explore the holiness of sex, we'll go back to the beginning in the

Garden of Eden. There we will embark on the journey of discovering what was on the mind of the Holy One as He gave the gift of sex to the first couple. But first it's important to understand where we've been in our own lives and where we are now. We need to sort through all that we've learned about sex, both true and false, so that we can return to the garden and learn the complete truth about sex.

And the foundation of that truth is that sex is holy.

THE LIES THAT HOLD US BACK

I don't know anyone who, when first learning about sex, was taught that it is holy. I certainly was never taught that. Like any teenage boy, I wanted to learn a lot—and I mean *a lot*—about sex. It seemed that junior high health class would be the ticket. However, in typical Texas fashion, my football coach was also my health teacher. In full crimson-faced embarrassment, Coach Smith gave us a hurried "how Sammy Sperm meets Elizabeth Egg" lecture. And that was it.

Convinced there was more, I turned to my "well-educated" peers. These teenaged experts shared a great deal of "adolescent sexual wisdom," the most important being that girls want to be ogled and grabbed. This made sense, considering our assumption that girls existed primarily for the enjoyment of boys. I was amazed at how much I was learning.

Imagine my surprise a couple of years later when, after I had become a believer in Christ, my new girlfriend handed me a copy of *I Loved a Girl*,[3] a book on Christian dating and sexual relationships. The author, Walter Trobisch, had obviously *not* spoken with my football buddies. Suddenly, my previous education was being challenged by ideas such as women should be respected as God's creation, Christians should save sex (and petting) for marriage, and—a really new idea—God designed, created, and gave the gift of sex to husbands and wives to be enjoyed. Really? God was the One who made sex fun? Orgasm was His idea? I must have been absent the day Coach Smith taught that part.

And yet, even in my burgeoning Bible-based sex education, the idea of sex being something more than a uniquely special way for a husband and wife to share their love was still absent. The only time I heard the terms *holy* and *sex* used together was in a spoof when Robin the Boy Wonder cried, "Holy sex, Batman!"

THE CULTURE OF SEX

We've all heard much on the subject of sex. In fact, we hear way too much. It's rare that we watch a movie that doesn't have its steamy scenes or at least thinly disguised sexual innuendo. We are surrounded by books that deal with every aspect of sexual dysfunction, technique, fantasy, and exploitation. Even a quick trip to the grocery store brings a deluge of magazine covers that taunt us about sex and our assumed incompetence in this area.

Our sex-saturated culture worships bodies, focuses on individual pleasure, and glorifies sex outside of marriage. Comedians and radio shock jocks rise to fame and fortune by pandering to our basest impulses. Women learn from the industry of "female appearance" that the key to getting a man is a perfect body—and the willingness to show a lot of it. Advice columnists remind us that by the "third date you should be ready and willing to have sex."[4] Cartoon heroines for kids are drawn with twenty-inch waists and forty-four-inch busts, and according to *U.S. News & World Report,* pornography recently took in more than $8 billion in one year.[5] Sadly, television has become "the leading sex educator in America today," showing sex between unmarried partners twenty-four times more frequently than between spouses.[6]

As a culture, we've decided that when it comes to sexuality, knowledge leads to fulfillment. In the popular 1970s book *Everything You Always Wanted to Know About Sex But Were Afraid to Ask,* author David Reuben stated: "The more you know about sex, the more you can enjoy it."[7] From the likes of Drs. Masters and Johnson to the Kinsey Institute, the phases and causes of orgasm for both men and women have been studied, documented, filmed, and analyzed. We know of the G-spot, multiple orgasms, and dozens of erogenous zones. (I know. Men think they have only one.) Sex therapy and medical science can cure impotence, premature ejaculation, and an assortment of vaginal muscle disorders. We know how it all works, and we think we know how to make it all work even better. And yet studies show overall sexual satisfaction is continuing to decline.

In short, we are more sexually informed than ever. We can take advantage of therapy and medical treatments not available to previous generations. And we have free access to more sexually stimulating material than at any time in history. But despite all of this knowledge, people are more sexually empty, more sexually frustrated, and more sexually lost than ever before. We must ask why.

SEX AND CHURCH HISTORY

Let's look at how we got here. Theologian R. C. Sproul observes that "throughout the history of the Church, some have expounded on the notion that sex within marriage is merely tolerated by God for the sake of procreation," and some have even concluded "that God regards sex as intrinsically evil."[8] That view is a long way from sex as a beautiful, holy act that invites the presence of God.

Additionally, some in the history of the church have regarded sexual pleasure itself as a consequence of sin. According to this view, before Adam and Eve ate the fruit that God had forbidden, sex wasn't part of the scenario. Instead, the knowledge of good and evil gave them sexual awareness.[9]

If this view is true, then any expression of sex, even within marriage, becomes sinful. Life in a monastery would be the only God-honoring alternative for any of us. Along these lines, Saint Augustine believed that sex was the vehicle for the transmission of original sin.[10] Borne out of his own confession that he couldn't find happiness, no matter how great his "indulgence in sensual pleasure," Augustine concluded that all sexual pleasure must be evil.[11]

Christian belief in the sinfulness of sexual pleasure went on for centuries. Only relatively recently did believers arrive at the idea that the pleasure associated with sex is a good thing. However, Jewish believers came to this conclusion much earlier. Rabbi Shmuley Boteach points out that the rabbis have always made female orgasm a moral obligation of the Jewish husband. In the Jewish tradition, "No man was allowed to use a woman merely for his own gratification."[12] Christendom has struggled a lot more with the "pleasure" side of the sexual equation. Thirteenth-century theologian Thomas Aquinas and church leaders John Calvin and Martin Luther all agreed that God had created sex for reasons besides procreation. However, they also viewed sex as "disorderly"[13] and never seemed to tread very long or dive very deeply into the controversial waters that sexual pleasure might actually be a gift from God.

Boy, have things changed.

Look through any directory of Christian resources and you'll find a book on sex or at least a book on marriage that includes a chapter on sex. (That chapter is easy to find. It's always the last one.) Even for believers, sex is a hot commodity. Still, the Christian world changes slowly.

In the late 1970s, Dr. Ed Wheat's book *Intended for Pleasure* gave Christians a great technical guide to sexual intimacy, and it did much to break the assumption that Christians shouldn't enjoy sex. However, by the time this book came out, *Everything You Always Wanted to Know About Sex But Were Afraid to Ask* had been on people's bedside tables for almost ten years, and the movie version, a Woody Allen comedy, was a major Hollywood hit. And when the Christian world finally published Wheat's candid book on Christ-honoring sexuality, it was wrapped in cellophane and stocked on the top shelf in Christian bookstores. The unavoidable message was that we may have a personal relationship with the Creator of sex and marriage, but we're still awfully embarrassed about what He created.

Today, many have heeded the advice of Dr. Howard Hendricks, author and Christian educator: "We should not be ashamed to discuss what God was not ashamed to create."[14] Since Wheat's groundbreaking work, a tidal wave of information on Christian sexuality has expounded on the premise that sex *is* for pleasure. We've come a long way from the days when sex was simply a wife's marital duty. But there's still more.

UNDERSTANDING THE HOLINESS OF SEX

I enthusiastically agree that God wants us to enjoy sex, but godly sex is so much more than just fun. And many followers of Christ are once again poised to be left behind while nonbelievers dabble in this truth. Many people outside the church are discovering that sex is much more than merely a physical act; it has a spiritual component. They are realizing that the deeper connection of sex goes far beyond simply understanding how to overcome sexual dysfunction. It goes way beyond technique and physique. This deeper dimension is experienced when we move past pleasure as a goal and instead seek intimate connection—not just with our bodies but also with our souls. Some are finding that when sex has a clear spiritual and emotional component, the sexual union holds a deeper meaning and therefore offers deeper pleasure. But without a relationship with the Creator through Christ and a full understanding of His purposes for sex, these people fall short of the encounter of oneness that God intended for us. They miss the core truth from which all other sexual truths flow. And that truth is that sex is holy.

Sex was created, inaugurated, and blessed by the source of holiness, God Himself. Before sin entered the world, God gave sex as a divinely unique and extraordinary gift to the original couple to share and enjoy with each other, to celebrate their oneness. Sex is holy as well because it is in sex, in the full unity of both male and female, that the full image of God is represented.[15]

We see this in the creation story. In Genesis 2, we read of the creation of Eve:

> The LORD God said, "It is not good for the man to be alone. I will make a helper suitable for him."…
>
> Then the LORD God made a woman from the rib he had taken out of the man, and he brought her to the man.
>
> The man said,
>
> "This is now bone of my bones
>   and flesh of my flesh;
> she shall be called 'woman,'
>   for she was taken out of man."
>
> For this reason a man will leave his father and mother and be united to his wife, and they will become one flesh.
> (verses 18,22-24)

There is much for us to learn in this first brief description of making love (verse 24). God created Eve not only to be a person distinct from Adam, but also to be the fulfillment of Adam. Adam named her *woman* (*issa* in Hebrew) because she was taken from *man* (*is* in Hebrew). These words indicate that she was *in essence* the same as the man. Taken in context with the description in Genesis 1:27, "So God created man in his own image, in the image of God he created him; male and female he created them," we learn that it is in the union of both woman and man that the full image of God is displayed.

Man, before the creation of woman, was somehow incomplete (see Genesis 2:18). God responded to this incompleteness by creating a "helper suitable" for the man (Genesis 2:20-22). The writer of Genesis knows, as he declares in verse 24, that as a man is united with his wife in sexual intimacy, they will again become one flesh, one flesh that celebrates their love and their relationship with each other. So the man, who was alone without the woman, and the woman, who was created out of the man, are separate entities until they come together in sexual union. That's when two bodies and two souls join to become, once again, one flesh. That is when a man and woman together most fully represent the image of God, which was breathed into them when He gave them life at Creation. This is a marvelous truth. Our Creator God, who is three persons in one Godhead, created a man and woman who become one flesh in sexual union, fully representing the God who created them and gave them His image.

It is important to note that this truth about sex doesn't mean that unmarried persons are somehow less representative of the image of God than those who are married. It does mean that the fullness of God, His *complete* image (albeit marred in our sinful state) is not fully represented by a lone individual. It is found only when women and men are together in community and communion in the body of Christ. That body, made up of individuals, represents God's image. Together, we represent His fullness. And that togetherness of male and female is most fully expressed in the holy state of matrimony as celebrated in the oneness of the one-flesh union. A holy act indeed.

THE SACRAMENT OF SEX

In the book of Leviticus, God commanded that certain items be consecrated for use in religious rituals and in acts of worship. These were made holy because they were set apart for special use in the worship of the Almighty.

Likewise, sex is holy because it is central to a sacred act of worship. It might seem odd for me to say this, but sex is holy just as the celebration of Communion is holy.

Christians celebrate Communion as a reminder of God's new covenant with us, our adoption into His family as sons and daughters, which is sealed by the blood of Jesus. This new covenant allows us, as believers, to enter into the holy place and the presence of God (see Hebrews 10:19). Because of Christ, our sins no longer prevent us from enjoying intimate communion with God.

Likewise, sexual intimacy should be celebrated regularly as a reminder of the covenant we made with our mates on our wedding day, the day that God joined us together. Sex is a celebration that allows us to enter into a holy place. Sex is holy in that the depth of love that can be experienced between a committed husband and wife brings honor to their Creator, the God who created them and their love for each other.

And sex is holy for yet another reason. Paul describes this holy aspect of sex as a great mystery, a mystery that, because of Christ, has now been revealed. That mystery is that the intimacy represented in the sexual union of a believing husband and wife is a representation—is, in fact, *the* representation—of the intimacy between our Savior and us, referred to as the bride of Christ (see Ephesians 5:31-32). Sex is holy because in the oneness of a human groom with his bride, the oneness of the groom, Jesus Christ, and His bride, the church, is represented.

In more ways than we can fathom, sex is holy.

But Is All Sex Holy?

It's impossible to discuss the holiness of sex without wondering about certain types of sex—the demeaning, the violent, and the exploitative expressions of sex. Surely they're not to be considered holy, are they? The short answer, of course, is no. But the existence of unholy sex doesn't mean that all sex is unholy. There seems to be a universal principle at work in the world that the things that have the greatest potential for good, if misused, also possess the greatest potential for evil.

For example, money has a tremendous potential for good if, as God's stewards, we use it to further His kingdom and to minister to the needs of others. Money also has a huge capacity for evil, serving as the motive behind theft, lies, and murder. Likewise, the family has a phenomenal potential for good as the chief agent for the socialization of children into the Judeo-Christian ethic and a great place for love and laughter. But families can also be a source of much evil when children are neglected and abused. Marriage also has the ultimate potential for good. Given by God to cure the problem of loneliness, it can give us strength, purpose, comfort, a sense of mission, and a place to celebrate love. But at the same time, marriage has produced a seemingly infinite amount of pain in the history of the world through abuse, selfishness, and divorce.

And sex has this same potential for good and bad. Sex provides the hope for good far beyond what most people dream or imagine. It can provide physical pleasure, to be sure, but it is also a way of communicating tenderness, compassion, caring, and love. It is a way of showing our most intimate connection with our mates and a way of showing God's intimate communion with us. But untold millions have also been devastated and even destroyed, either emotionally or physically, through the evils of sex. This evil that is associated with sex comes from the abuse of God's gift, not from the gift itself. God intended sex to be loving and pleasurable, not a source of heartache and destruction. The experience of holy sex is a gift to those who know the One who made it so. It is made no less holy because many have failed to use the gift according to God's created design and intent.

Still, the idea of experiencing sex as something that is holy might be difficult to accept. We may believe that sex is just a little too dirty and disorderly for God to be a big part of it, that it is too steeped in selfishness to be a way to experience God, or that there is just too much shame and pain in sex for God to be honored. Those ideas come in part from regarding human sexuality as being on the same level as sex between animals. In our culture's sexual obsession, we've become comfortable talking about sex as a natural bodily function, as something on the same level as going to the bathroom and not as something that, like breathing, is a part of our lives that affects all aspects of our life.

Seeing sexuality in such a compartmentalized fashion has caused us to discuss sex more as an activity that can be brought under submission. But our sexuality is much more than just a part of us. We are, to our core, sexual beings. Our sexuality affects everything we do, and everything we do affects our sexuality. We may deny this truth, but we can't escape it. But our quest to compartmentalize and regulate our sexuality in an attempt to understand its function and maximize its pleasure has actually caused us to minimize much of its God-intended joy.

For years in the world of counseling, marriage therapy and sex therapy have been considered two different fields of expertise focusing on two different sets of problems. The implication is that most sexual issues can and should be treated separately from the rest of the marital relationship (if there is even a marriage at all). The problem with this approach is simple: It doesn't work! You can't fully and adequately understand God's gift of sex apart from God's gift of marriage.

The attempt is similar to taking the main hard drive out of a computer and then expecting it to do the work of the whole computer by itself. I'm not a techie, but I know that a computer needs all its components to be connected before it can perform its proper functions. This point was driven home to me after I replaced the CD-ROM in the family computer only to have the whole machine fail to boot up when I was done. After two hours of installing and reinstalling both the old and new drives, followed by an hour and a half of on-hold Muzak at tech support, I heard a computer wizard sounding all of twelve years old ask me, "Is your hard drive plugged into the mother board?" "Sure," I replied, "I never touched it." "Well, why don't we check it anyway?" *What's this "we" stuff, Kimosabe?* I thought. Well, lo and behold, it wasn't plugged in. In jostling things around, I had inadvertently unplugged the hard drive. As soon as I plugged it in, the problem was solved. Likewise, when we remove sex from the context of marriage—even more, when we remove sex from the realm of the holy—we have unplugged the hard drive from the human relationship.

In the separation of sex from the marital relationship, we've taken the hard drive out, set it on the table, shown it to everyone, explained how it works, and then asked people to enjoy it. Even more devastating is that we haven't completely embraced our sexuality (that part of us that enjoys sex and sexual things) as a healthy part of our spirituality (that part of us that longs to know God). As such, people keep trying to get the hard drive to work all by itself, but it never does. A hard drive that is unplugged from its computer will never fully do what it was designed to do. Sex, unplugged from marriage and our spiritual selves, will never do what it was designed to do.

The separation of our sexuality from our spirituality causes the sexual pain and evil that pervade our world. When engaged in without God by people without an understanding of the holy, sex becomes an object whose only purpose is a biological sensation or procreation. As a biological urge, all sex sooner or later falls victim to the law of diminishing returns—

something that gives us a certain level of pleasure today will produce a lower level of pleasure tomorrow. God didn't design sex to be merely an urge or impulse. And He didn't intend that the excitement would wear off after only a few years.

Prayerfully consider this fact of creation: God created you as a spiritual *and* a sexual person. Spirituality enriches our sexuality. And sexuality doesn't exist in a vacuum, isolated from the rest of our being. A sexually spiritual person is not an oxymoron.

SEX AND GRACE

Plenty of authors are discussing the spirituality of sex. Your local bookstore is bulging with books on the Kama Sutra, sensual massage, and Tantric sex—all an effort to achieve spiritual sex without acknowledging the God of the Bible. Our world seeks a sexual high that lasts, delivering a new and better level of fun. However, the world's varied and creative approaches ultimately come up short because they don't acknowledge the One who created sex; they all fall prey to the law of diminishing returns.

Similarly, people from all across the faith map are seeking to synthesize their spirituality with their sexuality. It's time that disciples of Jesus did the same using the truth of the Scriptures. Ironically, we don't hear much about the spirituality and the holiness of sex from the community of Christian believers. It is this community that should understand the spiritual aspect of sex better than anyone, since we're the ones who have received the gift of grace. It is grace, God's free and undeserved gift of love and forgiveness that, through the blood of Jesus, has allowed you and me to enter into His presence and have a personal relationship with Him. And it is that same grace that allows us, as wives and husbands, to enter into the realm of the holy—through the celebration of His gift of sacred sex—and have the most intimate relationship with our mates. Grace is the one thing that can overcome the sin and the hang-ups that have prevented sex from being holy and sacred for many, many couples.

The fall from grace in the Garden of Eden that allowed sin to enter the marriage relationship introduced shame, which marred sexual expression between husband and wife. But the death and resurrection of God's Son allows us, through grace, to enter again into the original holiness that sex was created in. As Paul wrote to the Romans, "For just as through the disobedience of the one man [Adam] the many were made sinners, so also through the obedience of the one man [Jesus] the many will be made righteous" (Romans 5:19). Sin has affected us all, and it has certainly confused us sexually—just as it did Adam and Eve. But by and through God's grace, we can experience the true holiness of sex.

It's time for Christians to bring the idea of sex and holiness together. M. Scott Peck, in his book *Further Along the Road Less Traveled,* writes that "sex is the closest that many people ever come to a spiritual experience. Indeed, it is because it is a spiritual experience of sorts that so many chase after it with a repetitive, desperate kind of abandon. Often, whether they know it or not, they are searching for God."[16] In other words, the world's quest for meaningful sex is also a quest for meaning in life—for God.

Rabbi Shmuley Boteach states that sex is "as religious a subject as a discussion on belief in God."[17] The sexual unity of a husband and a wife, he believes, demonstrates the unity of God with all of His creation. "It is for this reason," he states, "that Judaism has always identified sex as the most holy of all human endeavors."[18]

As believers who worship the God of Abraham, Isaac, and Jacob, we have been given the privilege of encountering sex as the most holy, most intimate, most loving way we can connect with our mates. It is the celebration of the unity, the "becoming one," which is a stated biblical result of marriage. It is the proof and promise of the end of loneliness, the stated biblical reason for the creation of marriage. It is standing upon holy ground.

Yes, sex is holy.

QUESTIONS FOR CONVERSATION

Set aside a brief time to talk with your spouse about the holiness of sex. Share your thoughts and feelings on some of the following questions.

1. What do you think about the idea of sex being holy? Does this idea make sense, or is it difficult for you to believe? Why? Discuss any barriers to your ability to see sex as holy.

2. Genesis 2 shows that Adam and Eve were incomplete without each other and that their need for an intimate relationship with another person was not a sin. In what ways does that truth change the way you view your marriage? your feelings of loneliness? Are there times that you are afraid to tell your mate that you need him or her (not selfishly) or that you are glad that God gave your mate to you as a gift? If so, what do you think is the source of that fear?

3. Do you separate your spirituality from your sexuality? (Are you taking the hard drive out of the computer?) Does it make sense that at our core we are sexual beings and therefore must integrate our sexuality into the rest of our lives? Why or why not? What can the two of you do to begin to make sex a more spiritual celebration?

4. What change in your attitude toward your sexual relationship has come with your new or better understanding that sex is a holy endeavor? What can you and your mate do to treat your sexual intimacy in a way that is deserving of something that is sacred and holy?

5. Share with each other and with God your commitment to learn to experience your love in a more holy and God-honoring way.

Chapter 2

The Mystery of Oneness Revealed

What You Didn't Know About Sex Can Be the Best Thing You'll Ever Learn

> If, at first, the idea is not absurd, then there is no hope for it.
>
> —ALBERT EINSTEIN

I was watching my oldest son's football practice when I was reminded of something that I hated about football back when I played. It's the training technique of requiring the whole team to run a lap because just one kid jumped offside. One player makes a mistake, and the whole team suffers. This exercise underscores the point that, in a team sport, what each player does affects the entire team. I understand why it's done, but I'd be happy to let the kid who can't count run all by himself.

I have sometimes thought that Adam and Eve should have had to run laps all by themselves too. After all, they ate the forbidden fruit, not me. They messed up all by themselves; don't they deserve to suffer the punishment alone? Why can't the rest of us start out in the Garden of Eden and get our chance to do things right?

Well, I suppose there are a lot of reasons. First, it only takes about two nanoseconds for me to be reminded that when it comes to sinners, "I am," in the words of the apostle Paul, "chief" (1 Timothy 1:15, KJV). I would've failed in the garden as well (maybe even sooner than the brief six hours that Saint Augustine believed elapsed between the Creation and the Fall!). Second, because of the nature of sin and its consequences, Adam and Eve—as sinners—had no choice but to give birth to sinners. Two imperfect beings can't produce a sinless one. We're all sinners.

The other side of the coin is that we all, to some degree, experience God's grace. Every woman and man is loved by God whether we deserve it or not—and none of us deserve it. We can all experience the beauty of a sunset and the joy of laughter. Believers and nonbelievers alike can encounter the thrill of love, marriage, and having children. Every individual experiences God's gifts through what theologians call "common grace."

The gift of sex is, by common grace, something that can be enjoyed by people whether or not they know the One who created this gift. The physical pleasure, and the opportunity to create new life through the process, is available to all humanity by God's common grace.

However, sex presents to those who journey into its spiritual depths an opportunity for a much deeper experience. Sexual intimacy, even for the atheist, is by God's design a spiritual experience. That may sound absurd, but the words of Albert Einstein at the start of this chapter give me hope. The truth is that it's not possible to separate sexuality from spirituality. However, it's only those who have a saving relationship with God through Christ who can enter the exhilarating and ultimately fulfilling depths of the sexual experience. In other words, Christians are the only ones who can fully grasp and benefit from the holiness of sex.

"So," you may ask, "how is it that women and men who profess little or no belief in God still experience sex as a spiritual act?" Well, that's a mystery.

ENTERING THE MYSTERY

The difficulty of entering this mystery and understanding it is demonstrated almost daily in my counseling office. Sarah first came to see me at the urging of her husband, Michael.[1] It's always an interesting experience when one spouse sends the other one to therapy to "get fixed." I typically insist that the absent spouse join us in future sessions since it's difficult to do coronary repair when only half of the patient is on the operating table. In Sarah's case, her answer to my first question made it obvious that we needed Michael present—even though he didn't see it that way.

When I asked what I could do to help, Sarah stared at the carpet. "I just don't like sex very much," she said quietly. She had come to my office prepared to answer a series of questions about her personal history that might lead to a diagnosis of her "problem." At least in her husband's mind, Sarah was the one with the problem.

Instead of probing her background, however, I asked Sarah about her beliefs. "Sarah, what do you believe is the purpose of sex?"

With a quizzical look, she answered, "I don't know if I'm sure what I believe. Obviously it's to have children and it's something men need, but beyond that, I don't know. Right now I can take it or leave it." Sarah was expressing a sentiment that, sadly, is held by many women.

I didn't immediately tell Sarah that part of what she assumed to be true was wrong. Men do not, in fact, have a life-or-death need for sex (more on this in chapter 6). But I did ask if she thought sexual intimacy was something God wanted her to enjoy. Her response: "I know I'm supposed to say yes, but I'm not sure about that either." At this stage of her life, the only reason Sarah could think of to have sex was to keep her husband from complaining, whining, or moping around. Beyond that, the big reasons for sex were a mystery to her.

UNLOCKING THE MYSTERY

In the Bible, the term *mystery* has nothing to do with solving a riddle or getting to the answer in a whodunit novel. In Scripture, a mystery is something that was previously unknown but now has been revealed. God explains these matters if He wants and when He wants and to whom He wants.

In Ephesians, Paul wrote about two mysteries that God has made known. The first was the incredible place in the church now afforded to the non-Jews; the second was the incredible role that sex has in marriage. Both speak to the holiness that God confers on these now-revealed mysteries.

Concerning the first mystery, Paul states that not only could Gentiles be saved along with Jews, but that through the Messiah, Jews and Gentiles together would make up God's church (see Ephesians 2). To the Jewish mind, it was unthinkable that Gentiles could ever enjoy an equal standing as sons and daughters of the Most High. But God had declared this nearly incomprehensible news to be the truth.

As for the second mystery, Paul sets up its revelation by first instructing wives and husbands about the countercultural, God-ordained ways in which He desires them to treat each other. Marriages lived in the light of Christ are to be about extreme sacrifice, submission, respect, and love. Paul writes:

> Submit to one another out of reverence for Christ.
> Wives, submit to your husbands as to the Lord. For
> the husband is the head of the wife as Christ is the head of
> the church, his body, of which he is the Savior. Now as the

church submits to Christ, so also wives should submit to
their husbands in everything.

Husbands, love your wives, just as Christ loved the
church and gave himself up for her to make her holy, cleans-
ing her by the washing with water through the word, and to
present her to himself as a radiant church, without stain or
wrinkle or any other blemish, but holy and blameless. In this
same way, husbands ought to love their wives as their own
bodies. He who loves his wife loves himself. After all, no one
ever hated his own body, but he feeds and cares for it, just as
Christ does the church—for we are members of his body.
"For this reason a man will leave his father and mother and
be united to his wife, and the two will become *one flesh*."
This is a *profound mystery*—but I am talking about Christ
and the church. However, each one of you [husbands]
also must love his wife as he loves himself, and the wife
must respect her husband. (Ephesians 5:21-33, emphasis added)

Paul uses an analogy to describe life for a husband and wife who are
unified in Christ. But this is no casual illustration, no case of marriage
merely being "like" something else. Instead, Paul declares that the relationship between husband and wife is, in effect, the full representation of
Christ's relationship with us, His church and His bride. As one commentator put it, "The marriage relationship is now set out as being a reflection of
the relationship between Christ and his church. This is to raise it to an
unimaginably lofty level."[2]

And how is this lofty marriage relationship a true reflection of Christ's
relationship with us, His church? That is the mystery! Paul is stating that
what everybody from Adam and Eve, to Abraham and Sarah, to Hosea and

Gomer (my favorite Old Testament name) did *not* know was that their marriage relationship—more particularly the oneness of their marriage relationship—was always meant to exemplify the oneness of Jesus, the Bridegroom, with His bride, the church.

This oneness is spiritual, to be sure, but it is much more than that. In our current era, we often emphasize the mystical oneness that occurs in marriage and that should be displayed emotionally and spiritually. But there is also a clear physical dimension to this state of oneness as well. In the Old Testament, to be "one" meant to have sexual relations. Paul carries this concept over to the time of Christ when he writes, "Do you not know that he who unites himself with a prostitute is one with her in body? For it is said, 'The two will become one flesh'" (1 Corinthians 6:16). By quoting Genesis 2, where we find God's description of the first marriage, Paul emphasizes the oneness that sexual intimacy creates. Sex makes two people one whether they are married to each other or not, whether they want it to or not. Sex and oneness can't be separated.

Which brings us back to the mystery. Paul isn't telling husbands in the Ephesians passage to love their wives *as if* their wives were their own body. He is stating that husbands should love and serve their wives as Christ does the church because they are, in fact, "one body with themselves."[3] A man's wife *is* his own body. The wonderful, life-changing, mind-boggling truth is that marriage—more specifically, the sexual relationship within marriage—actually makes two people become one, and that oneness has been given the holy role of representing the intimacy between Jesus Christ and His bride.

Leading up to the mystery, Paul has used the words *Christ* and *the church* in the same sentence four times: Christ is the head of the church (verse 23); the church submits to Christ (verse 24); Christ loves the church and gave Himself up for her (verse 25); Christ feeds and cares for the church (verse 29). All of this is part of the intimate oneness that Christ shares with His bride. But that oneness in its essence is created through a saving grace relationship, begun in God's love and only culminated with Christ (Ephesians 2:4-5).

In the same way that Christ loves the church, husbands and wives are to love and care for each other, they are to submit to each other, putting the other's needs above their own. It is part of the oneness of their marital intimacy. But the essence of that oneness is created through their sexual intimacy. Far from being a product of pure animal instinct, sex melds two people together in a way that makes them one body—a singular entity that actually portrays not the mystical, but the real presence of God.

A QUESTION OF IMMORALITY

All of this raises a very thorny question: Does illicit sex—any sexual encounter outside the bonds of marriage—represent the intimacy of Christ and the church? Does an act of sexual immorality actually represent the real presence of God?

Let's take a look at the biblical teaching. First, the Bible tells us that God is omnipresent: He is everywhere all of the time (see Psalm 139:7-8). So in response to the question "Is God present when sex occurs between those who are not married to each other?" the answer is yes. His heart is broken, but He is there, just as He is present when we lie or act ungenerously or gossip.

But what about the teaching that sex represents the unity of Christ with His bride, the church? In 1 Corinthians 6, we see the consequences of sexual immorality and its effect on oneness and the body of Christ. Paul writes:

> Do you not know that your bodies are members of Christ himself? Shall I then take the members of Christ and unite them with a prostitute? Never! Do you not know that he who unites himself with a prostitute is one with her in body?

For it is said, "The two will become one flesh." But he who
unites himself with the Lord is one with him in spirit.

Flee from sexual immorality. All other sins a man commits are outside his body, but he who sins sexually sins
against his own body. Do you not know that your body
is a temple of the Holy Spirit, who is in you, whom you
have received from God? You are not your own; you were
bought at a price. Therefore honor God with your body.
(verses 15-20)

When believers have sex with a prostitute (or anyone who isn't their
spouse), they are not just becoming one with the sex partner. They are also
uniting the body of Christ with the other person. And that is part of the
reason why this sin produces such grave consequences. (Paul points out in
verses 18 and 19 that sexual sin is a sin against the temple of the Holy
Spirit.) As believers, if we have sex outside the bonds of marriage, we have
dishonored God with our bodies by becoming one in the wrong way.

However, within the protective boundaries of the wife-husband relationship, sex brings incredible honor to God. But for the oneness that is
established in sexual intimacy to be truly representative of the mystery of
Christ and the church, it must include—albeit marred by our selfishness—
the kind of sacrificial love described in the verses leading up to Ephesians
5:32 where Paul declares the mystery. Marital sex creates oneness. Marriage
is holy as husbands and wives humbly and earnestly seek to let their whole
love fully represent Christ's love for His bride.

And it has been that way from the beginning.

God-Honoring Intimacy

As a marriage counselor and teacher, I often have wished for a New Testament book entitled *Peter's Letter to Believers Living in the State of Matri-*

mony. I choose Peter because we know he was married. (He had a mother-in-law—I'll skip the jokes.) I'd also pick Peter because he's such a likable character, able to say everything right at one minute and tripping all over his tongue and goofing up the next. Reminds me a lot of some husbands I know (and one I know real well). And husbands like us could use a book where we could find "Hints for Having a Happy Holiday at the In-laws' While Keeping Your Wife Happy Too." I know it would be a big seller.

This imagined letter about the state of matrimony would take us back to the Garden of Eden as the incomparable model for marriage, and it would provide the direct, unambiguous teaching that would put all of us confused spouses on the path to marital fulfillment. We'd get a faint glimpse of the beauty, harmony, and fun that a wife and husband are supposed to experience together. And then, as I was pondering this possibility, I realized that we don't need directions from a new and improved book of the Bible. Jesus Himself already returned us to the Garden, the place where we can learn all we need to know about God-honoring marital intimacy.

Jesus opened our eyes to the truth about marriage in Mark 10, when the religious teachers tried to get Him to commit blasphemy. They thought that if they could trick Jesus into speaking against the laws that God gave to Moses, they could use His statement to get rid of Him. The test in Mark 10 centered on questions of marriage and divorce. The leaders were wondering whether it was okay for a man to divorce his wife and, if not, why Moses gave them permission to do so. Here's Christ's answer:

> It was because your hearts were hard that Moses wrote you
> this law.… But at the beginning of creation God "made
> them male and female." "For this reason a man will leave his
> father and mother and be united to his wife, and the two
> will become one flesh." So they are no longer two, but one.

Therefore what God has joined together, let man not separate. (verses 5-9)

To correct their mistaken ideas about marriage, Jesus took them back to the beginning by quoting Genesis 2:24: "For this reason a man will leave his father and mother and be united to his wife, and they will become one flesh."

Jesus first of all explains why Moses had given them this exception clause: because their hearts were hard. Throughout the Bible, people who don't want to follow God's laws are said to have hard hearts; it's another way of saying that they were selfish and wanted to follow their own desires. In Deuteronomy 24, where this "divorce clause" is found, Moses was addressing an existing situation and was, by God's direction, simply trying to prevent the people from heaping evil upon evil. The Mosaic provision was an attempt to limit the extensive and painful consequence of a practice of divorce that already existed.

As such, the teachers coming to Christ were not wondering whether divorce was acceptable—they fully believed that it was. They were simply representing two schools of Jewish thought at odds over *when* divorce was acceptable. In response to their query, Jesus applied a common technique of period debate. He invoked the superior authority of an earlier, and thereby weightier and loftier, truth to bolster his argument. It's hard to get any earlier, weightier, and loftier than God at Creation. Jesus referred to the greater principle: the way God intended it to be when He first created Adam and Eve. It's what is called the creation ordinance: the laws that were built in when God formed the universe.

THE MEANING OF "ALONE"

John Sailhamer, a professor of Old Testament, points out that whenever God stated that part of His creation was "good," it was only good to the degree that it related to and benefited His crowning creation, Adam and Eve.[4] The universe that was created during the first five days all led up to one major climax: the arrival of God's image in the form of two uniquely created human beings. All that was "good" was for them.

The familiar first "not good" is that Adam was alone, and this aloneness was not good even before sin entered the picture. It is incredibly important for us to grasp the circumstances of this problem. Adam is alone, and he is still a perfect creation of God. No sin was blocking his intimacy with the One who had formed him from the dust, and yet he was alone, and it wasn't good.

So how did God respond? Did He chastise Adam for being lonely and then tell him to get over it or to just trust Him more? Did he give Adam three drinking buddies and a television so they could watch *Monday Night Football* together? Okay, then what about two wives, a wife and a mistress, or a succession of wives? Or how about this: God could give Adam lots of stuff and a busy schedule to dull his senses and help him forget that he was lonely.

None of those was part of God's answer to the loneliness problem. God's solution for the pain of being alone was Eve.

God provided a solution for loneliness, the result of a situation He had created in the first place. God created Adam's loneliness because He knew beforehand that He had the perfect solution. Then God revealed to Adam the mystery of why he existed in a state of perfection and yet felt alone: Adam was lonely because, without his wife, part of him was missing. Even though Adam was created in God's image, without Eve he didn't yet *fully* represent God's image. The work of creation wasn't complete until God formed Eve from Adam's rib.

Genesis 1 gives us the overview of God's creative process. In Genesis 1:27 we read, "So God created man in his own image, in the image of God he created him; male and female he created them." Professor Richard

Davidson of Andrews University has pointed out that "it has been rightly observed that discussion among theologians over this passage has largely focused on the meaning of man's creation in the 'image of God' and has almost entirely ignored the further affirmation that humankind is created male and female."[5] The writer of Genesis, by God's leading, pointed out in the discussion of being created in God's image that the creation was "male and female." Adam was not the only creature who bore God's image.

Theologian Karl Barth saw the last part of verse 27 ("male and female he created them") as the exposition of the first two parts. To Barth, that statement meant that "man-in-fellowship as male and female is what it means to be in the image of God."[6] Modern-day theologian Walter Brueggemann further makes this point when he states, "Humanity in community is male and female. And none is the full image of God alone."[7] Pastor and author Stephen Sapp writes that the full image of God "refers to neither Adam alone nor to Eve alone, but only to the two of them together, to the 'them.'"[8]

None of this means by any stretch that unmarried people are somehow less representative of the image of God. A married man or woman is no more or less the bearer of God's image than a single man or woman. But it is in community of male and female that the full image of God is represented. Unmarried people have full access to the community of believers, where the fullness of God's image is represented in the body of Christ.

However, it is in the oneness of marital sexual intimacy—in the reunion and rejoining of the male and the female—that the fullness of God's image finds its highest expression. That is why it's only in the intimacy of the sexual relationship that God declares that "the two will become one flesh" (Mark 10:8). The attributes of both male and female are necessary for completing the image of God that is borne by all humanity.

In the gospel of Mark, when the religious teachers questioned Jesus about legitimate reasons to break up a marriage, Jesus referred His questioners to the unity that a husband and a wife create. He reemphasized this point by repeating that "they are no longer two, but one" (Mark 10:8). Furthermore, Jesus reminded them that the oneness, the unity, was created by God Himself, not by a merely physical act. What God has joined together is a vision of Himself. As such, it is holy. As a picture and symbol of God's image, the joining of male and female in marital sex is the closest we come to entering the Holy of Holies. Let me explain.

INSIDE THE HOLY OF HOLIES

The Bible tells of a number of ways that God makes His presence known. He spoke to Moses from a burning bush (see Exodus 3:4). He moved with the Israelites in the desert as a cloud and as a pillar of fire (see Exodus 13:21). He spoke to Saul the persecutor in a blinding light (see Acts 9:4). But the abiding image of God's presence, the most sacred and hallowed place of God's presence, was the interior of the temple in Jerusalem, the Holy of Holies. In Exodus 26, God gave specific instructions to the Israelites as to how to make the curtain that would separate this Most Holy Place from the rest of the temple. To the children of God, the Holy of Holies was not merely a location; it was the very presence of God Himself.

When Adam and Eve sinned, the consequences of their act not only drove them from the Garden of Eden and caused God to station an angel to prevent their reentry, but their sin also kept them from enjoying open fellowship with God. In Moses' day, God had His children construct a place where He would, again, meet with them. However, because the Hebrews were in the same condition of sin as Adam and Eve had been, only one representative of the people, the high priest, could actually enter into the Holy of Holies and be in God's direct presence. Immediately outside the Holy of Holies was an area known as the Holy Place. Here, the priests of God were to come daily to commune with God and tend the altar. By God's instructions, however, the Holy of Holies was to be entered into only once a year—and then only by the high priest. On this day, known as the Day of Atonement, the high priest entered into the presence of the Creator to offer sacrifices (to make atonement) for the sins of the nation of Israel. God's commands regarding this annual sacrifice and the consequences of violating the rules that governed it were so severe that the high priest would actually enter into the Holy of Holies with a rope tied to his foot. If by chance he died while in God's presence, the rope would enable the other priests to drag him back through the curtain, knowing that if they physically went in to retrieve the body, they, too, would die.

In the New Testament, the gospels of Matthew, Mark, and Luke report that at the moment of Jesus' death, the curtain that had separated the Holy Place from the Holy of Holies was torn in two, from top to bottom. This tearing indicated that God Himself had removed the barrier that had kept His children from His presence. The writer of the book of Hebrews builds on this event and explains yet another mystery: Jesus Christ, as the supreme High Priest, has provided the ultimate sacrifice for the sins of the people. Through His death, all who believe in His resurrection and therefore belong to Christ can enter into God's direct presence.

> Therefore, brothers, since we have confidence to enter the
> Most Holy Place by the blood of Jesus, by a new and living
> way opened for us through the curtain, that is, his body,
> and since we have a great priest over the house of God, let
> us draw near to God with a sincere heart in full assurance of
> faith, having our hearts sprinkled to cleanse us from a guilty
> conscience and having our bodies washed with pure water.
> (Hebrews 10:19-22)

The stunning good news is that we have a High Priest, Jesus Christ, who has made the sacrifice for our sins so that we can freely enter into the actual presence of God. Because of God's amazing grace, what was barred to Adam and Eve is freely offered to every one of us.

Since God's grace has given us the opportunity to walk again in His presence without sin's being a barrier, doesn't it also make sense that, as husbands and wives, we can also by His grace return to the same type of pre-sin intimacy that Adam and Eve enjoyed? To be sure, we're still sinners and we'll never achieve a perfect marriage. However, we do have a High Priest whose death ripped apart the curtain that separated us from God. Therefore, as wives and husbands who together represent the full image of God, we can experience the holy and worship-filled life of a couple that God has joined into one. We can return to the garden because of the cross of Christ.

The mystery is revealed! The children of God who have been separated from their Creator may once again walk in oneness with their God, in the holy communion established solely by the blood of the Lamb. And wives and husbands, in their sexual oneness, may walk again in the garden of His presence.

THE TRUTH ABOUT SEXUAL STRUGGLES

Where does this lofty truth leave Christian couples who are struggling with their sexual relationship? Let's go back to the story of Michael and Sarah, the couple in my counseling office. Michael thought that his wife and her low sexual desire were the problem. Sarah thought sex was primarily for procreation and for the pleasure of her husband. They had missed the tremendous blessing that God wove into the very fabric of the sexual relationship.

From the day she got married to the day she entered my office, Sarah had slowly constructed a sexual model and finally concluded, "Men need sex to live, and it's my job as a wife to provide it." The idea of sex being a mutually enjoyable, emotionally and spiritually intimate encounter was foreign to her. Sarah viewed sex as a duty, similar to paying bills, cleaning the house, or even breast-feeding an infant. It doesn't matter how you feel about the task. It simply needs to be done.

Women who nurse their babies often go through a stage of feeling that their breasts are not their own but are simply there to provide food for a hungry infant. "I feel like a milk cow" is a sentiment I have heard more than once. This is not to say that they don't enjoy nursing, nor are they complaining about feeding their child. It's simply that they develop the feeling that someone else owns their body.

Many women feel the same way as they relate sexually to their husbands. It seems that their breasts, their vagina, their whole body does not belong to them; those parts are simply there to fulfill a task for an over-grown child who needs them. And contrary to many nursing experiences, those women *don't* enjoy this demand.

In my counseling office I've encountered dozens of women who share Sarah's view of sex. It's just one more thing on their to-do list, an obliga-tion that keeps someone else happy. These women want to just get sex over with so they can get on to something else—like sleep. Devoting a few minutes to sex is preferable to enduring several days with a pouting hus-band. It's not hard to understand Sarah's feelings about sex: "I can take it or leave it."

Michael attended the next counseling session with his wife. It was a lights-on experience for him when he learned that their sex life was actually causing a creeping separateness and even resentment between him and his wife. It was a lights-on revelation for Sarah when she realized that sex was designed to be so much more than a physical encounter and that it has a higher goal than procreation or even orgasm. It was a lights-on moment for both of them as they began to understand that sex is holy and is intended by God to be a celebration of intimacy with God as well as with each other. As a result, their attitudes toward sex started to change.

As Michael began to cherish the holiness of their marriage, he started to factor God into their sexual experience. He became openly thankful for the privilege of entering into God's presence through the oneness of sex. In his gratitude, he started to share regularly with his bride what was on his mind and in his heart. He brought a renewed tenderness and patience to their bedroom. He expressed his awe that God had brought Sarah into his life and that they could enjoy the intimacy and fun of sex. As Michael grew in his understanding of the sacredness of sexual intimacy, he no longer expected his wife to agree to sex on demand. Rather, he began to prepare both himself and his marriage for sex by creating love and intimacy with his wife.

By inviting your mate inside your mind, your heart, and your spirit, you're working to create the wholeness of oneness that gives sex its meaning and, ultimately, its true pleasure. It's important to remember that we don't open up with the goal of getting more sex. Instead, we do so because it's what God's wants us to do—and the result is true intimacy.

Michael's new openness in sharing his heart had a dramatic effect on Sarah's self-diagnosed "low sexual desire." Knowing that Michael no longer saw her as a sex object with two breasts and a vagina, but as a person with whom he could share in one of the greatest mysteries of all time, changed everything. When her husband shared from his heart, even to the point of weeping as he expressed his thanks for how much his wife and his Lord loved him, Sarah became sexually aroused for the first time in years. Within a few days she initiated a night of sexual celebration, something that hadn't happened in a long, long time.

That's one result of practicing sex as a holy act. Knowing how much God values our sexual connection, knowing that He wants us to enjoy each other, and knowing that sex is holy and sacred, we stop thinking of our sexual relationship as an isolated experience. Instead, the oneness of sex takes a place of honor in our marriage.

Husbands and wives know intuitively that sex is much more than simply an act of physical release. When we view sex as a sacred act, a holy place in God's presence, marital sex takes on a profound nature. As those to whom God has granted the gift of marriage, we couples realize that we are one flesh with our mate. We are no longer alone. And every time we make love, we are ushered into the presence of God.

And this is a wonderful mystery indeed.

QUESTIONS FOR CONVERSATION

Take time to discuss the mystery of sex with your mate. The following questions will help.

1. Share your reaction to the idea that marital sex is a representation of the relationship between Christ and His bride, the church. What do you feel about God being present in a mysterious yet real way in every sexual encounter? How do these biblical principles alter your view of sex?

2. Have you ever thought about the fact that it takes both woman and man to fully represent the image of God? Share with each other all the ways you can see that truth reflected in your own differences within your marriage.

3. Consider the story of Michael and Sarah. What aspect of their relationship mirrors your own? Can either one of you relate to either character? Share the similarities and dissimilarities between them and you and how the changes they made may benefit your marriage as well.

4. When has your love for each other been representative of Christ's love for His church? In what ways has your love fallen short? (Remember, we've all fallen short.)

5. Are you committed to exploring together this mystery of oneness? Share that desire with each other, expressing your fears as well as your sense of excitement. Then say a prayer, committing yourselves to pursuing the spiritual mystery of holy sex.

Chapter 3

The "Big O" Is Not Orgasm

Entering the Promised Land of Sexual Fulfillment

> Marriage is an adventure, like going to war.
>
> —G. K. CHESTERTON

Brenda kept apologizing for the feelings she was sharing. She didn't want to hurt her husband, Kevin, but she'd kept her thoughts hidden for too long. Now, for the sake of her marriage, she was glad that everything was finally coming out. Kevin was sitting next to Brenda in my counseling office, but he wished he could be somewhere else.

"I know I'm not supposed to exaggerate," Brenda began, "but it seems that every time we're alone, Kevin makes some sexually suggestive comment aimed at getting me to have sex with him. I feel like he must spend his days coming up with new lines to try to get me to say yes. And if it's not a comment, it's a grab. I can be cooking or doing the dishes, and he'll come up behind me and plant both of his hands on my breasts. A hug would be great. But he can't seem to touch me without it being in an erogenous zone."

Now Kevin really wanted to be somewhere else.

Brenda assured me that she didn't hate sex. "I can get aroused, and sometimes I even have an orgasm. But the more Kevin pushes, the less I want to have sex. The more he talks about 'doing it,' the more I feel that sex between us is just that: a cold, impersonal 'it.'"

"And have you begun to feel like an 'it' too?" I asked.

"Yes. Yes I have."

Now Kevin wanted *me* to be somewhere else.

Brenda's story is another sad example of how much we're missing in our sex lives. By losing sight of sex as a holy act, we're depriving ourselves of the richness and deep satisfaction that God designed it to provide. Since sex is invested with so much spiritual meaning, that should affect the way we approach our moments of sexual intimacy—but how? When we acknowledge the truth that sex on God's terms is sacred, we can stop fighting about frequency, positions, and who initiates it. Here's why.

BEYOND RECREATIONAL SEX

If you ask the average person in the pew to identify the primary purpose of sex (and if you manage to avoid getting hit with a hymnal), he or she will most likely say either procreation or recreation. Of course, both are rich blessings of sex. But the essence of sexual intimacy can never be enjoyed, nor can true and lasting sexual fulfillment occur, until a wife and a husband grasp the truth that the number-one purpose of sex is neither procreation nor recreation, but *unification*. And I don't mean just the unification that is inherent in physical oneness, but also the relational unity that is celebrated, created, and re-created throughout a couple's married life. This unification is the celebration of the soul-deep bond that is present when a couple knows and experiences the certainty that they are together, permanently, for a divine purpose. They know their expression of love is meant to represent the loving relationship of Jesus and His church. They know that their life together has meaning that is far greater than simply sharing a house or bearing children.

People can have sexual intercourse without having a long-term commitment or even a close relationship with each other, and oneness still occurs. In those circumstances, however, the oneness is not lived out. The thoroughgoing oneness of holy sex is lived out in the shared life and purpose that permeates the relationship outside the bedroom. The experience of oneness that gives sex its soul-touching meaning is created by having a shared life—emotionally and physically—in *all* areas of your relationship. That shared life, that relational oneness, is what can make sexual intimacy everything it was meant to be. In turn, sexual oneness makes the rest of your marriage more fulfilling.

The sex that Brenda and Kevin shared was accomplishing a number of things, but relational oneness wasn't one of them. Everything about their sexual encounters, both in bed and out, was a battle for the achievement of their individual goals and desires, not for their mutual benefit. Brenda became focused on self-preservation and maintaining her self-respect. Kevin was absorbed in his physical impulses, so he remained focused on orgasm.

There are plenty of Kevins out there, so it's important that we grasp this truth. Underline it, highlight it, or put big stars by it, but get it down: *Whenever we make orgasm the goal of sex, we will fail to experience godly sex.* In other words, the "Big O" of sex is not orgasm; it's oneness.

SEXUAL UNION

People who believe that procreation is the primary purpose of sex often base their interpretation on the familiar words "be fruitful, and multiply" from Genesis 1 (KJV). The proponents of procreative sex believe this is the Bible's first mention of sex. However, Genesis 1 and 2 do not lay out a series of events in chronological sequence. The first chapter of Genesis is best understood as an overview of the entire Creation story. Then, in chapter 2, God returns to the crown of His creation and highlights it by discussing the surroundings, reasons, and interactions of the two human creations who together represent His image. In that detailed description, we find the purpose of sex defined as "they shall be one flesh" (Genesis 2:24, KJV). Oneness, quite apart from procreation, is of prime importance.

Jewish tradition continues to uphold this interpretation. According to Rabbi Shmuley Boteach, Orthodox Jews have not embraced the "extreme secular view that sex is for fun and pleasure [only]. Rather, Judaism says that the purpose of sex is to synthesize and orchestrate two strangers together as one." To Jewish believers, "sex is the ultimate bonding process."[1] In Hebrew, the word *yadà* is often used to describe the sexual relations between a man and a woman. It means to "know by observation, reflecting, and experiencing."[2] It is the word used when Scripture states that "Adam knew Eve his wife; and she conceived" (Genesis 4:1 KJV). Sexual intercourse, by God's description, is the way of knowing and experiencing another human being in the most intimate way possible. This "knowing" is what melds two strangers into one.

A wonderful example of this is a Dutch slang word for sex, *naaien*, which literally means "sewing." Two pieces of material are put on top of each other and then attached in a way that will "keep them secure and fastened to each other long after the sewing is over and the weaver is gone."[3] This idea of being sewn together in sex is a useful image for picturing the unification that still respects our individuality. Husbands and wives don't dissolve together into one shapeless blob. However, they are intricately and intimately sewn together by God in such a way that man should "not separate" them (Matthew 19:6). Oneness joins us permanently without destroying our individuality.

Further, oneness lasts beyond the immediate act of sexual intimacy. In marriage, we celebrate a oneness that has existed since the last time we were together and will continue after our sexual interlude. We don't experience sexual joy for twenty minutes and then walk away unchanged. We are now one with our mate. Orgasm delights for a moment; oneness lasts a lifetime.

Marital sex works as a circle of oneness. Having been joined by the oneness of intercourse, that union should affect every other part of our relationship. Being unified in all areas of marriage—feeling cherished, valued, respected, and cared for—creates within us a desire to become one with our mates again through sex. Sex creates oneness, and oneness fosters a climate that naturally leads to more and better sex. When we feel one with our mates, we want to be united with them.

SOUL-TOUCHING SEX

Have you ever wondered why, every time you stand in the grocery store checkout line, dozens of magazines with sex-related articles are screaming for your attention. The easy answer is that we live in a sex-obsessed, "sex sells" culture. But I believe there is another, far different reason. I see these articles as attempts to sell us the lie that if we put their advice into practice, we'll obtain a sexual high that we never dreamed was possible. The magazine editors know we aren't satisfied sexually, so they tempt us with their "new" advice. They want us to believe that we'll finally enjoy true sexual satisfaction if we buy their magazine.

Why do people keep falling for this stuff? It's because couples are looking for sex that satisfies more than just their temporary physiological urges. People are seeking a form of sex that touches the deep yearnings of the soul. But looking for a solution in secret techniques doesn't address those deeper yearnings. Trying to find soul-satisfying sex without first seeking oneness is similar to men's trying to fulfill their sexual urges with pornography. The fantasy provides short-lived pleasure that always leaves the user wanting more. And when a man does get more, he is left wanting even more. Far from providing satisfaction, the object of sexual desire only creates more desire.

Brenda and Kevin knew about seeking sexual pleasure in the absence of oneness. Brenda felt that she'd been reduced to the status of a sex object. She didn't feel that Kevin really wanted *her;* he just wanted her body—and only certain parts of that. Sex didn't feel like creating and celebrating love; it felt like "doing it."

Since Kevin was sitting there, saying nothing, I introduced the idea of sex as a mysterious, holy endeavor designed to create intimate oneness. Then I asked Kevin to describe the spiritual intimacy that he and his bride shared. He stumbled around looking for the right words and, frustrated, finally landed on, "You know, I believe in God and all, but I don't believe that just reading the Bible will make us closer or give us answers to our problems. Even more, Brenda really tries to push this stuff on me, and I kind of resent it because then she ignores our sex life. She comes to bed all excited about this stuff, but I don't see her excited about sex."

I wanted to yell "Bingo!" Kevin had stumbled upon the key that would unlock sexual fulfillment in his marriage.

ONENESS IN WORSHIP

As my lovely wife likes to tell women, "Don't read *Glamour* or *Cosmopolitan* to find out how to improve your sex life. The Bible is a much better place to start." And men, if you want to do something that your wife will find sexy and sensual, try this simple act of foreplay: Pray with her. I don't mean saying grace before dinner, nor do I mean asking God to bless Grandma and Grandpa and your dog Skippy. I mean *really pray with her.* Bring before God your fears, your failures, your hopes, and your dreams. And pray for your wife, for the challenges and demands she faces each day, for her worries, for her strength. Then thank God for her beauty, her charm, her friendship, and her faithfulness. And praise God for giving you the privilege of sharing in His beautiful gift of sexual intimacy with her. It might sound crazy, but praying together opens doors to intimacy that you never even suspected were there.

I must add the caution that great sex is not the goal of praying together—it's part of the result. Just as the goal of being tender, considerate, supportive, and emotionally open is not hot sex but rather relational intimacy, a man should not pray with his wife thinking that when it's over he'll be sexually rewarded. Praying together simply and profoundly deepens the intimacy that will in turn deepen the sexual experience when it occurs.

I imagine some of you are thinking, "Enough with the theory. Let's start talking about how to deal with things like infrequent sex, lust and temptation, and boredom in the bedroom." We'll address these and other common sexual struggles beginning in chapter 4. However, let me remind you that this book is about understanding the Creator's purpose for sexuality. Only within that understanding can the most troublesome sexual issues truly be resolved.

Such was the case for Kevin and Brenda. As we talked about God's desire for couples to experience true oneness, they realized that sex should be a spiritual experience. This realization was the beginning of significant growth. Kevin became more open to changes that needed to occur in order to increase their emotional intimacy, which in turn made Brenda more willing to explore their sexual intimacy. Together, they grew in their appreciation of God's gift of marriage. Sexual intimacy became a way of expressing and sharing the love that they were both thankful for. And since a spirit of love and thankfulness is part of the experience of worship, Brenda and Kevin even began to see how sexual intimacy, viewed in the light of mysterious holiness, provided new pathways into the praise and adoration of their Creator.

I once saw a cartoon where a groom is kneeling by his bed on his wedding night, his wife lying in wait for him, and he is praying the familiar mealtime prayer: "Bless us, O Lord, with these, Thy gifts, which we are about to receive from Thy bounty through Christ the Lord. Amen." It's funny. It's cute. And it should be true—laughter and all.

THE OTHER "O" DOES MATTER

While standing on the truth that the "Big O" of sex is, from God's perspective, oneness and not orgasm, it is important to discuss the fact that orgasm is an integral part of God's design for sex. Just as we asked the question, "Why sex?" we must also ask, "Why orgasm?" Again, God could have done things any way He wanted. But since He created us (especially women) with body parts whose sole purpose is to provide intense physiological pleasure, we must ask if the physical pleasure of sexual intimacy stands on its own or if, in fact, there is more to it.

As any sexologist (and most couples) will tell you, orgasms are powerful. But they are not, I believe, powerful in and of themselves. If they are experienced simply as a physiological release through masturbation or in partnership with anyone other than your spouse, they will, as we have discussed, ultimately fail to satisfy. But when they are experienced at the hands (and body) of our marital partner, the one we truly love and cherish, their power is great indeed. The bodily movement of our whole-life partner, moving in conjunction with our own body, reflects the very essence of why God established this act of oneness to occur with physical bodies between a husband and a wife.

Why is it that holding hands with brothers and sisters in Christ while standing in a prayer circle is simply a bond of fellowship, while holding hands with my wife can both comfort me *and* thrill me? How is it that a kiss on the cheek from a good friend is simply a warm hello, while a kiss on the cheek from my wife can send me soaring? Is it not because these latter experiences are received from the one with whom I am most intimately connected in body, mind, and soul?

And if just holding hands with our mates can give us a thrill, just imagine what sacred sex can do! At the point of orgasm for both women and men during sexual intercourse, each partner *must abandon control of their own orgasm to their partner at the same moment they feel most vulnerable.*

That is why people who struggle with control issues and with trusting their mate often struggle with achieving orgasm; they will always be on guard, not abandoning themselves to the love and care of the other. But it is in that gift of abandoning control to our mates and trusting them in our most vulnerable state that the full union of physical oneness is most deeply experienced. It is there that we find sacred sex at its most powerful manifestation. The extreme intensity of the orgasmic experience is due to the fact that it is had *with* our God-given mate.

That, by God's design, is a truly powerful experience, indeed.

A NEW FORM OF WORSHIP

As we noted earlier, sex is the closest that many people ever come to a truly spiritual experience. Even more, sex is the closest that many people ever come to worship.

Recently I asked for feedback from a group of couples who had heard me teach about sex as a holy endeavor. As you can guess, the comments were fun and fascinating. The most common reaction was "I'd never thought of sex like that before." The second most frequent response was that describing sex as a form of worship seemed sacrilegious. Put bluntly, they thought I was out of what was left of my oversexed mind.

I realize that saying that sexual intimacy can be a form of worship sounds like a guy trying to come up with a new line to get his wife into bed: "Hey, honey, want to go to church tonight?" I don't recommend this approach, since it's more likely to get you a night on the couch. However, if we acknowledge the extraordinarily high worth that God places on sexual intimacy and if we understand that sex is a holy experience that represents Christ and the church, then seeing it as a form of worship is not that big a leap—but only if we understand worship.

The *New Bible Dictionary* states that worship "originally referred to the action of human beings in expressing homage to God because he is worthy of it. It covers such activities as adoration, thanksgiving, prayers of all kinds, the offering of sacrifices and the making of vows."[4] In the Old Testament, *worship* primarily referred to activities that God's people performed to acknowledge that He was, in fact, the one true and holy God. In our worship services today, much of what we do through song, sermon, and prayer is aimed at affirming the sovereignty of God and offering our thanks for the gift of His Son, Jesus.

However, the *New Bible Dictionary* goes on to state that in New Testament times, "'worship' is misunderstood if we assume that the major element is what humans do or offer to God."[5] Instead, worship consists of two elements: our acknowledgment of what God does for His people and our response to what God has done as demonstrated by how we live our lives. In other words, our lives should continually reflect our thankfulness for His grace. As Paul urges us in Romans 12:1, we are, "in view of God's mercy, to offer [our] bodies as living sacrifices, holy and pleasing to God—this is [our] spiritual act of worship." In short, we should worship God continually with our entire lives.

The *Holman Bible Dictionary* carries this thought even further by defining worship as a "human response to the perceived presence of the divine, a presence which transcends normal human activity and is holy."[6] The point is illustrated with the Old Testament story of Jacob's dream about a ladder rising up to heaven.

> When Jacob awoke from his sleep, he thought, "Surely the LORD is in this place, and I was not aware of it." He was afraid and said, "How awesome is this place! This is none other than the house of God; this is the gate of heaven."
>
> Early the next morning Jacob took the stone he had placed under his head and set it up as a pillar and poured

oil on top of it. He called that place Bethel [which means
"house of God"], though the city used to be called Luz.
(Genesis 28:16-19)

The commentator in the *Holman Bible Dictionary* notes that "before
the dream, the place had only been a stopping place reached by sunset
(Genesis 28:11), but when he [Jacob] awoke it had become a holy place.
The holy presence of God had penetrated into ordinary (profane) space in
a way which had aroused acute awareness on the part of a human being.
The sacred (holy) and profane are united in an experience of worship."[7]

Worship, then, can be as simple as affirming or confirming the presence of God. It is admitting that the Lord God is truly present in the activities of our lives.[8] Worship is experiencing the holy God of the universe in
the mundane activities of everyday life. It is worshiping the presence of the
sacred amid the profane.

THE SACRED AMID THE PROFANE

If you endured a philosophy of religion course in college, you'll remember
a discussion of the apparent paradox of finding the sacred, that which is
holy, in the midst of the profane, that which is ordinary. If you pull out
your copy of Mircea Eliade's *The Sacred and the Profane: The Nature of Religion,* you'll read (after blowing the dust off the cover), "For modern con-
sciousness, a physiological act—eating, sex, and so on—is in sum only an
organic phenomenon.... But for the primitive, such an act is never simply
physiological; it is, or can become, a sacrament, that is, a communion with
the sacred."[9] Though Eliade might label us "primitive," our discussion
about worship being an awareness of God in everything fits with the idea
that nothing is ever "simply physiological."

However, the idea that God is present and can even be honored by the
sexual act sounds primitive at best—and absolutely wrong-headed at worst.

How can something that has become so trivialized and created such unmitigated devastation actually be divine? In other words, how can an act that has been so profaned ever be sacred? The answer is simply "Because it is." It is precisely because sex *is* so holy and sacred that it can be twisted in such a way that it appears very unholy. The ancient Jewish mystics were adamant about the fact that the loftier the concept, the more it was subject to abuse.[10] The almost universal degradation of sex doesn't nullify its inherent sacredness.

When we profess with our mouths that Jesus is Lord and believe in our hearts that God raised Him from the dead (Romans 10:9), we encounter the holiness of the true High Priest, the One who has gone before us and who brings us into the real presence of all that is sacred. And when we acknowledge that God created sex and gives it to couples to celebrate and commemorate the oneness of Christ and the church, we become intensely aware of the sacredness of the act of married love and we worship the One who gives it.

Since sexual intimacy creates and re-creates oneness—a oneness that is intended by God to be permanent—it is only within the permanent and sacred commitment of the marriage relationship that sex can be holy, good, and right. Understanding that we have been given the privilege of participating in the holy act of sex, we then experience the sacred—the presence of God Himself as He gives us His grace.

SEX AS A CHANNEL OF GRACE

Sacraments have long been a part of the church's worship of Christ. By definition, sacraments are sacred reminders of God's grace to us. They contain both a vertical and horizontal element, as is illustrated with the symbol of the cross. In the sacrament of Communion, we share horizontally our spiritual relationship with the entire body of believers; we share vertically our spiritual relationship with Christ Himself. Sacraments, then, are an outward celebration of an inward relationship. They are a celebration and an experience of God's unimaginable grace.

I'm not proposing that sexual intercourse should be ordained as one of the church's sacraments (though I'd probably get a lot of supporters if I did). But if sex is holy (and it is), and if sex can be an act of worship that acknowledges God's presence (and it can), and if sex is a means by which we create oneness, sustain oneness, and are in fact "made one" by God's decree (and, yes, it is), then is it not also true that sexual intimacy can be a way of experiencing God's grace here on earth? Even more, is it not a way that I can offer an experience of God's grace to the one I have committed myself "to love and to cherish till death do us part"? Yes, I believe it is.

And what that means is this: Sex is not about me and what I want, and it is not about you and what you want. Sex is about sharing an experience that neither one of us deserves. Grace is the absolutely free, absolutely undeserved, absolutely amazing gift of enjoying God and having access as His adopted children to all of the riches of our Father, the King. As wives and husbands, we are joint heirs together of the grace of life (see 1 Peter 3:7). And sexual intimacy, as experienced in and by God's design, is certainly an undeserved journey into the treasure house of the divine. It is a sacred reminder of our vertical relationship with Christ and His church as celebrated in the horizontal intimacy of a husband and a wife, fellow heirs of God's grace.

A PLACE TO REMEMBER

A couple of times a year, Amy and I have the privilege of participating in a marital enrichment retreat called Marriage Makers. It's based on the truth that, by God's design, we must work to make a great marriage happen. One of the fun things we do on these weekends is insist that couples go on a picnic together. We pack them a picnic basket, give them a blanket, stuff in a list of possible things to talk about, tell them they have four hours, and send them out to find a spot where they can enjoy their time. Without fail, the weekend evaluations list this as one of the highlights. The couples are doing something fun that they don't often make time for.

In the Song of Songs, the great Old Testament love story that offers further proof of God's holy and fun view of sexuality, we find the story's lovers enjoying the beauty of God's creation in yet another way. In commenting on this, pastor and author Stephen Sapp writes:

> The Song [of Songs] is significant precisely in that it reminds us of a central fact...too often overlooked today, namely, the goodness of all creation, including man's [and woman's] physical body and [their] sexual nature. In its vivid descriptions of the body of the beloved, the love and sexual passion of the lovers, and the beauty of the country-side, there is no question that the Song is stating unequivo-cally that these are all intended and therefore good parts of God's purpose in creation, to be celebrated and not denied.[11]

In chapter 7 of the Song of Songs, the woman invites her husband on a journey to the countryside. She bids her lover:

> Let us go early to the vineyards
>> to see if the vines have budded,
> if their blossoms have opened,
>> and if the pomegranates are in bloom—
>> there I will give you my love. (Song of Songs 7:12)

Now, there aren't too many men who would turn down an invitation to this picnic! What is more important, however, is the point that Sapp is making. These lovers, desiring to share their love, are not only enraptured by each other and by the prospect of making love, but they also are motivated and entranced by the beauty of the world that God has given them to enjoy. In their lovemaking, they are intensely aware of the majesty of God's creation, and they are, in fact, celebrating that creation.

I can appreciate what these lovers felt being together in the midst of God's glorious creation; I have always been awed by the wonder of places like ocean shores or mountain peaks. Even more since Amy and I met each other when we were working at a Christian youth camp in the magnificent Rocky Mountains of Colorado. I know, I know, romance is not supposed to happen among the camp staff, but hey, with us it did. We still enjoy visiting there, not only because it's a tremendous experience of the majesty of God's creation, but also because it's a vivid reminder of the place where God began the process that led to our own experience of marital oneness.

From that wonderful, memorable beginning (which did not, I should note, include the outdoor affections of our Old Testament lovers), we have not only ventured through various stages of marriage's Promised Land, but we have also had our share of experiences of wandering in the wilderness. At times sexual intimacy has been truly an "us" experience, and we have indeed encountered the divine in worship. Sadly, at times sex has also been a monument to "me," drifting off to sleep selfishly upset by my mate's desire for closeness without having it lead to sex. But our willingness to work at creating an "us" experience—often preceded by my saying, "I'm sorry. I was wrong. Please forgive me"—has brought us back, time and again, to the land of God's blessings. We have returned, as any repentant sinner ultimately must, to worship the ever-gracious God who made us one.

MARRIAGE'S PROMISED LAND

John Ortberg, author and teaching pastor at Willow Creek Community Church, writes:

True celebration is the inverse of hedonism. Hedonism is the demand for more and more pleasure for personal gratification. It always follows the law of diminishing returns, so that what produced joy in us yesterday no longer does today. Our capacity for joy diminishes. Celebration is not like that. When we celebrate, we exercise our ability to see and feel goodness in the simplest gifts of God. We are able to take delight today in something we wouldn't have even noticed yesterday. Our capacity for joy increases. [12]

Life, for the believer, is about genuine celebration. It is about understanding that, in the midst of pain and personal struggle, the God of the universe is with us, seeking to flood our existence with love and joy. But almost as common as the belief that Christians aren't to enjoy sex is the one that says Christians aren't even supposed to enjoy life. No way! God calls us to joy. He calls us to notice the simple, celebrate the good, and be thankful for all the blessings that come from Him. God calls us, even today, to enter the Promised Land.

And yet so many of us are afraid to go.

In his book *A Lasting Promise,* counselor and marital researcher Scott Stanley draws a wonderful analogy between the children of Israel standing at the edge of Canaan, the brink of the Promised Land, and Christians standing on the brink of God's design for marriage. [13] In the book of Exodus, God instructs Moses to send twelve spies into the land that God was going to give them. He wanted them to know that it truly was a place flowing with milk and honey.

When the spies returned, all of them agreed that the land was everything God said it would be. However, ten of the spies were scared because the people of the land were powerful. The other two spies, Joshua and Caleb, agreed that yes, the people were strong, but then they reminded the Israelites who was on their side, who had made the promises, and who it was that would lead them safely into the Promised Land.

Nevertheless, having heard the report of the ten weak-hearted spies, the people were afraid, and God did not allow them to enter the land. An entire generation missed out on the blessings that God had desired to give them. Stanley points out that many Christians never experience all of the blessings that God has waiting for them in the land of marriage because they are afraid to enter in. They fail to do the things that will let them experience and enjoy the fruits of the Promised Land of marriage.

This analogy also works for the adventure of holy sex. Very few people enter into a sexual relationship or experience it the way God intended it to be. We fall short of that glorious experience. Like the fearful Israelites, we, too, miss the blessings. Often, we don't even want to think about the gift of sex as sacred or holy because if we do, we'll have to confront the fact that we don't like or even want sexual intimacy. So we stand on the edge of the Promised Land thinking that life would actually be better back in the wilderness.

But the grace of God calls us forward. Fears may be screaming in your mind that this place of sacramental unity is one to which you can never go; the giants are simply too big. But just as God is explicitly present in the sharing of sexual love, He will also be faithfully present during your journey to get there.

We've been given the incredible opportunity to become one with another human being. We've been granted the incomprehensible privilege of representing the image of God, the Creator of the universe, in the intimacy of our sexual love. And we are called to worship Him "in spirit and in truth" (John 4:24) with our lives and with our love in the midst of all His magnificent creation.

I pray that you and your spouse will join together on this journey and be open to all that God has in store for you. I pray that you become two of the blessed few who have the courage, by God's grace, to enter into the blessings of the Promised Land of marriage.

QUESTIONS FOR CONVERSATION

Let these questions help you discuss the oneness that comes with God's gift of sex.

1. Have you bought into the lie that you are somehow sexually inadequate and therefore need a new technique (or even a new body) to be able to experience better sex? What do you think about the view, presented in this chapter, that true sexual satisfaction will only be found when you seek oneness above all else? Share with your mate how and why that makes sense to you, and discuss why it might be difficult to understand and live out.

2. If seeing sex as holy is a struggle for you, then seeing it as a form of worshiping God can really be a stretch. Still, according to the definitions of worship given in this chapter, does the argument make sense to you? Share with your spouse (being willing to laugh a little) how you feel about sex as worship.

3. Think about how often your pursuit of sexual intimacy has been focused on orgasm instead of oneness. In light of God's desire that we experience oneness, what changes do you feel you need to make in your thinking? Share with your mate some specific things that you plan to do in order to seek one-

ness above simply having sex. Suggest at least two ways that your spouse can help you in this process.

4. Have the two of you ever really prayed together? What prevents you from making this a regular part of your marriage? What would it take to make praying together a regular practice? Make a prayer plan—and then follow through.

5. Are you ready to enter into the true celebration of marital oneness? Take this opportunity to pray together and to commit to each other to go on this journey together. Ask God to help you every step of the way. He will; He promised.

Chapter 4

Naked and Unashamed?

What Unconditional Acceptance Will Do for Your Sex Life

> Every time a woman leaves something off she looks
> better, but every time a man leaves off something he
> looks worse.
>
> —WILL ROGERS

A number of years ago when I had an office at my church, a speaker for a women's retreat was given permission to use my office to change clothes for her presentation. No problem. Happy to help. The only trouble was that the folks who gave their consent and unlocked my office door forgot to tell someone—me—about the arrangement. So I came along, took my keys out, and then heard four sounds almost simultaneously: the click of my key going in the lock, the pop of the lock releasing, the creak of the door as it opened, and the scream of the woman as she leaped across my office, grabbed her dress from the back of one chair, and landed behind another. I can say this: The woman was fast.

Now, so you know, she was wearing a full slip when I barged in. Still, her immediate, almost innate reaction to hide from someone intruding on her while she was changing clothes was almost as quick as my retreat from my own office. Why is that?

There may seem to be several right answers, some dealing with such issues as modesty and privacy, but it seems that the most likely reason is simply this: Nakedness makes us feel shame. If that's true, though, why does the Bible make such a big deal about being naked and *not* feeling any shame? The person who wrote those words had obviously never had a stranger walk in while he was changing.

THE FIRST WEDDING PRESENT

Let's return to the scene of the world's first marriage and consider the first wedding present ever given. There are lessons to learn here about shame and how it affects marital intimacy. First, the wedding:

> But for Adam no suitable helper was found. So the LORD
> God caused the man to fall into a deep sleep; and while he
> was sleeping, he took one of the man's ribs and closed up
> the place with flesh. Then the LORD God made a woman
> from the rib he had taken out of the man, and he brought
> her to the man.
>
> The man said,
>
> "This is now bone of my bones
>   and flesh of my flesh;
> she shall be called 'woman,'
>   for she was taken out of man."
>
> For this reason a man will leave his father and mother
> and be united to his wife, and they will become one flesh.

The man and his wife were both naked, and they felt no
shame. (Genesis 2:20-25, emphasis added)

These two people hardly knew each other, yet they stood there wearing nothing and not experiencing even a glimmer of embarrassment. It has been assumed that Adam and Eve were unashamed because, at that time, there was no external standard for physical beauty. So who knew if they fell short of or surpassed that standard? Or maybe, since they were the very first man and woman, they *did* have perfect bodies.

Both explanations miss the point. Even if they were flawless human specimens, that physical condition had nothing to do with their complete freedom from shame. Their lack of shame was due to something else: It was due to their complete and total acceptance of each other, without reservation.

We have all probably heard Adam's response to God's provision of Eve ("This is now bone of my bones, and flesh of my flesh") read in a detached monotone. But somehow I don't think that's how Adam reacted when he was introduced to Eve. It's helpful to remember that he'd just watched a long parade of warthogs, hippos, orangutans, and every other type of creature walking past—and they all had dates. Now, feeling very much alone, he awoke to find not another furry, four-footed mammal, but a woman— a ravishing, delightful, completely naked woman. Now, how do you think he reacted?

As the old joke says, I think Adam's response was more like "Whoaaa! Man!" which is, of course, where we get the word *woman*. Think about it. We can watch grown, somewhat mature men scream, holler, slap hands, pat rears, bump chests, and pump their fists in the air when their team takes a little oblong ball across a white line on a field of grass, but we think lonely Adam's first response to a completely naked Eve was, "Well, okay. I suppose she'll do"? I don't think so.

In addition to noting Adam's enthusiasm, we need also to consider what he did *not* say: "Gee, God, thanks, but I would've preferred a brunette with smaller hips and larger breasts. And, Lord, you know I'm a pretty quiet guy, so if you would, don't have her need anything—like a lot of meaningless conversation—from me."

Adam's response was not only one of fanatic fervor, but also one of full acknowledgment that God's provision was everything he needed. He accepted his wife as God's magnificent creation and the fulfillment of his need, the end of his aloneness. And Eve received that gift of total, enthusiastic acceptance from the most important man in her life. The first wedding present was total acceptance of each other as God's perfect provision. Adam received his bride without reservation, with unconditional acceptance. That kind of reception is key to being naked and unashamed.

A CULTURE OF SHAME

Many who read Genesis 2 believe that this picture of total acceptance was unique to the first couple. I mean, how many of us have a spouse that was created by God *just for us?* Actually, if you sought God's leading when selecting a mate, then in a sense you *were* created for each other. Adam and Eve's experience is not all that unique.

But even if we buy into the "God brought us together" idea, there's still the "naked and unashamed" part to wrestle with. Most of us haven't devoted our lives to cosmetic surgery, starvation diets, or spending our every free hour in a gym. As a "regular" woman or man, neither do we benefit from the photo retouching expertise of a fashion magazine's art director. Our photos exhibit crow's feet, a receding hairline, and those extra pounds we've carried since last Christmas. Most of us are thankful that, in our culture, clothing is *not* optional.

But in a cruel irony, our consumer culture glamorizes the naked body while simultaneously making us feel ashamed of our own bodies. The female form is used to sell everything from SUVs to power tools. But that curvaceous yet anorexic (see the contradiction?) model is selling more than just tools and trucks. She's also convincing us that there's no way we can be satisfied with our bodies as long as we remain in the sorry state we're currently in. I'm a target of that message, and I'm a balding, aging father of three. It's even worse for women. If the rail-thin waif in the Calvin Klein ad sets the standard for physical attractiveness, how is any woman going to feel good about getting naked in front of her husband?

The thundering message of our culture is inescapable. If we don't start buying the right things and looking the right way—and soon—we're doomed to a meager existence of inferior personhood. The success of this sales pitch relies on our accepting the underlying assumption that we couldn't possibly be happy with how we look. And it's not just our looks we should be dissatisfied with, but also our allegedly routine approach to love-making. *You call that a sex life? If you don't take advantage of this special offer that will make you look years younger and a whole lot sexier, then shame on you!* And believe me, there's plenty of shame to go around.

FALSE SEXUAL GODS

What does all this have to do with holiness? Nothing that I can tell. Our cultural landscape reduces the holy act of sex to the superficial level of physical appearance. If we're worshiping big breasts, bulging biceps, and rock-hard bellies, then we've created an idol. Sadly, we're bowing down before a false sexual god rather than experiencing the liberation of personal intimacy and the sexual enjoyment that we were created to experience.

The Bible has one solution for those who've been seduced by false gods—whether it's a graven image or a cultural image of the perfect body. The solution is to destroy the idol. On the way to Canaan, the Hebrews were distracted by false gods. On our way to the Promised Land of holy sex, we've been sidetracked by the false promises of commercialized sex.

The graven images on the billboards and in the magazine ads have seduced us in more ways than we realize.

If we believe that our mate sees us as flawed, we'll enter into sexual encounters with each other fearing that we're displeasing to the one whose acceptance of us matters most. We'll feel like we're simply not enough. And if we believe that we could never be enough, we can't give ourselves to one another in a completely genuine way in holy sex.

"So what's the technique to overcome this shame thing?" you may be wondering. When it comes to shame, better sex techniques aren't the answer. The solution is found in creating an emotional, physical, and spiritual atmosphere of intimacy where sexuality and sensuality can be enjoyed to the fullest extent of God's intentions.

MIND AND BODY

When it comes to sex, our feelings of shame lead to all sorts of difficulties, both physical and mental. Somatic ailments, for example, are mental struggles that display themselves in physical symptoms, and it's easy to confuse the symptom with the cause. We assume that issues such as low sexual desire and responsiveness are physical problems or, more specifically, body problems. So we attempt to treat them physiologically with hormone treatments or behavioral techniques. But the truth is that many sexual dysfunctions originate in the mind.

I won't claim that if you apply the ideas in this chapter that you'll never again be nonorgasmic or will always find your sexual appetites in sync with your mate's. However, I do fully believe that arriving at the place of sacred sexuality actually eliminates many of the classic sexual problems. And giving and receiving the gift of being naked and unashamed is crucial if we are to enter fully into that sexual Promised Land.

Let's begin by asking a couple of questions. Ladies, how would you feel if one day your husband suddenly said, "Honey, have you ever considered getting breast implants? I'm really turned on by big breasts"? The next time your husband saw you topless, you'd be convinced that he found you somehow lacking, even inferior. While wanting to feel fully accepted by your husband, you'd end up feeling rejected—and ashamed.

Now a question for you husbands. How would you react if, while attending a social gathering, you overheard your wife talking to her friends about Tom Cruise? "He is *so* good looking. I don't care what the movie's about as long as he's in it. I could watch him all night long!" Would you immediately run out and join a health club and change to an acting career, or would you just stand there, silently hurt that it wasn't you that your wife was gushing over?

Both dropping hints about desired physical changes and showing undue admiration of someone other than your mate will break down your spouse's sense of being accepted. You may think of it as innocent banter or harmless joking around, but the Bible calls it out of bounds. The writer of Proverbs reminds us that, "Reckless words pierce like a sword, but the tongue of the wise brings healing" (12:18). We must ask ourselves whether our words bring healing to our mate's insecurities or whether they pierce them like a sword.

When I read the Scriptures, I notice that one condition for enjoying the riches of holy sex is that a person finds sexual stimulation in only one way: from enjoying the love of his or her mate and accepting that mate just as he or she is. Our mates should be the only ones we think of as being sexy, the only ones who get us hot, and the only ones we ever think about being intimate with. Jesus teaches us that just thinking lustfully toward anyone other than our mate is, in fact, a violation of our sacred marital covenant (see Matthew 5:28).

The cultural lies that convince us that great bodies are the secret to great sex rob couples of the fullness of sexual satisfaction. Being ashamed of our bodies in front of our mates will stifle any type of God-honoring sex.

Sexual fulfillment can't come in the absence of complete acceptance. And acceptance begins with a single-minded focus on your mate—just as he or she is.

A SHAMEFUL LIE

Shame is a problem that runs much deeper than our shape, our size, or the straightness of our teeth. Shame dates back to early childhood. Who doesn't have vivid memories of the pain caused by the taunts and jeers of classmates? No matter our social or economic status, our popularity or accomplishments, we all carry scars that come from being told we don't measure up. We still encounter people and events that make us feel less worthy, less deserving, and simply *less* than everyone else.

Men often balk at this truth, protesting that it doesn't apply in their case. If they've managed to accomplish much in their adult years, they like to believe that their conquests today outweigh their defeats of yesterday. If you're like that, let me ask a few questions. Does your wife know everything about you? Does she know all of your desires, every unbridled thought, everything you've ever done that you still regret? I didn't think so. Why not? Because of shame.

Shame keeps pain from the past active in our lives, and it prevents us from being fully open and vulnerable with our spouse. Shame is the false guilt that we feel over things in the past that we had absolutely no control over.

Guilt, in a healthy sense, says honestly, "I did something wrong." Guilt should motivate us to change and to avoid repeating the same poor choices. Guilt moves us to repentance before God. Shame, on the other hand, doesn't say, "I did a bad thing." Instead it says, "I am a bad thing. There is something wrong with me." Shame focuses on who we are, not a mistake that we made. The only apparent solution to shame is to run and hide.

What did our ancestors in the garden do after they sinned and God came looking for them? Adam tells God, "I heard you in the garden, and I was afraid because I was naked; so I hid" (Genesis 3:10). It's true that Adam and his wife had made a wrong decision and then acted in disobedience to God's commands. So they likely felt some honest guilt over their sin.

But their hiding indicates something more. They felt shame, which altered the way they viewed their nakedness. As marital researcher Scott Stanley points out, the first thing they did was cover up where they were the most different.[1] Their differences made them feel shame. Before, they were naked and unashamed, totally free in their relationship with each other and with God. Now, they recognized their nakedness and chose to cover it. Like the guest speaker changing clothes in my office, they dove for cover. Were they guilty? Yes, just as I am and just as you are. We've all fallen short of the glory of God (see Romans 3:23), and it is only by His grace through Jesus that our guilt can be removed. Adam and Eve's guilt separated them from God. Their shame separated them from each other.

And their shame didn't go away when they were banished from the garden. They took it with them, and it still infects us today. We experience it when we believe that we have unlovable parts and that we must not let others see what they are.

Shame affects the very core of marriage because it makes us feel inadequate in lovemaking. If I consider my body somehow deficient when it comes to pleasing my mate, then I'll never be able to enter into sexual intimacy in a completely open, free, and uninhibited manner. Shame erects a barrier to enjoying godly intimacy.

Shame forces us to act in opposition to what we need. Instead of desiring to find that person who will accept us for who we are, what we've done, and what we've become, we resolve to keep our secret parts secret. Since we're convinced that the person who will accept us despite the things we're ashamed of doesn't exist, we begin, as psychologist Dan Allender says, to hate that part of ourselves that is longing to be wanted and enjoyed.[2] If someone knew about those hidden parts that we deem broken or shameful, we're sure that person would abandon us. It's no surprise, then, that shame is so closely linked with nakedness. After all, shame fosters the belief that certain things about me must be kept hidden. We engage in sex, we may even in some ways be "making love," but we don't experience sex in a way that touches our souls. A brick wall of shame and self-condemnation keeps us separate.

For most couples, the lack of acceptance almost always involves the things that bug us about each other. It's one thing to say, "Honey, I'm bothered when you leave your dirty clothes lying all over the bedroom. It makes me feel like you think I'm your housekeeper, and I don't like that." In those types of situations, when two individuals truly care for each other, the "offending spouse" should change his or her behavior out of love for the mate.

However, it's an entirely different thing to say; "Why don't you think before you do such stupid things?" "Why don't you lose fifteen pounds?" or "I wish you were better in bed." Whenever we say things that attack our mate's personality, temperament, or preferences, we're not accepting him or her. Even further, whenever we complain about traits that are unchangeable, we're further adding to their feelings of shame.

THE SOLUTION TO SHAME

What can we do about the shame that prevents soul-touching intimacy? Let's go to the very core of the kind of sexual union we all long for. At the heart of this experience we find complete, total, absolute acceptance. Eve had no reason to doubt that she was everything Adam ever needed or desired.[3] What wife or husband could confidently say this same thing about feeling fully accepted today? Not many, I'm afraid.

Sexually, we try to compensate for our shame by learning new, exotic positions, increasing our frequency, or changing the shape of our bodies.

But those things are not going to solve the problem of shame. At the core of a soul-touching sexual union is the absence of shame, and we banish shame by accepting each other. No matter how much hair your husband has lost, no matter how many extra pounds your wife has gained, the basis for acceptance is the same for you as it was for Adam: It is believing that the mate God gave to you is everything you need in a life partner. You can choose to fully accept him or her as God's gift of grace to cure your loneliness and bless your life.

Acceptance is what gets us to the point of standing naked—physically, emotionally, spiritually—before each other and feeling no shame. Do we completely accept and praise our mate's bodies or do we make our mate feel inadequate or even ugly? In a world that has made us feel that parts of us are unlovable, do you create an atmosphere of tenderness and of complete acceptance of your mate? Have you offered your mate the gift of loving him or her without any condemnation? Have you experienced such acceptance yourself? If your relationship hasn't provided an environment that is free of shame, then you haven't experienced sexual intimacy in the way God designed it.

Since the concept of being completely naked and feeling no shame originated with God, it makes sense that getting back to that state begins with God. We must take the truth from our heads to our hearts that God knows everything there is about us, every thought, every failure, every shame-producing episode—and He still wants us to be His children. Romans 5:8 teaches us that God's love is demonstrated to us in that "*while we were still sinners,* Christ died for us" (emphasis added). God didn't wait until our guilt and shame were gone before He loved us. On the contrary, it was out of His love for us that He provided the path to set us free from guilt and shame by taking away our debt and "nailing it to the cross" (Colossians 2:14). His love for us isn't dependent on our acceptability.

Only when we know God's unconditional love for us can we offer that same gift to our mates. It's only then that we can experience intimacy with another human being as God designed it. As psychologist Larry Crabb writes, "We all need to be close to someone. Make no apology for your strong desire to be intimate with someone; it is neither sinful nor selfish."[4] Further, Crabb states that "the central truth that serves as the platform for Christian marriage…is that in Christ we are at every moment eternally loved and genuinely significant."[5]

Sounds great, but what does that have to do with shame? According to Crabb, we can be fully aware of those things for which we feel shame and still know that in God's scheme of things we are "at every moment eternally loved." However, Crabb's main contention is that "our personal needs for security and significance can be genuinely and fully met only in a relationship with the Lord Jesus Christ."[6] We must first find our significance in God. That means we don't base our significance on our good looks, our mate's beautiful body, or a successful sex life. To find genuine significance, we must first have our shame removed by the cross of Christ. We must first stand naked and unashamed before God. Only then will we begin to find the significance that lasts.

And then we must extend the gift by letting our mates stand naked and unashamed before us. When we experience the security and significance that come from knowing God's Son and when we experience His removal of our guilt and shame, we are hypocrites if we then fail to accept our mates. When we are criticizing them and pushing them to change because we believe those changes will make us happier, we are in effect putting ourselves in the place of God. And as others have said, people can make good husbands and wives, but they make lousy gods.

BETTER SEX THROUGH ACCEPTANCE

In my counseling practice, I frequently see female patients whose initial reason for therapy is a lack of interest in sex. In some cases, the reasons behind a low sex drive can be traced to issues of an overly strict upbringing or unpleasant sexual experiences in the past. In other instances, the lack of interest is one of the devastating consequences of being sexually abused. In still other cases, though much less frequently than most people believe, lack of interest is due to hormone imbalance of some kind. However, the vast majority of the female clients I see with low sexual desire suffer from a combination of two problems: a lack of understanding of the purpose and holiness of sex and an ailment I technically refer to as HD: Husbandus Dysfunctionus. In layman's terms, it's a nonaccepting, critical husband.

For a woman to know complete freedom in lovemaking and to achieve an incredibly intense orgasm, she must first feel completely accepted. I know many women can achieve an orgasm even when that level of acceptance isn't present, but that's because they have learned to manipulate their clitoris in a way that brings about a physiological response. That's not the type of sexual release I'm talking about. The profound adventure that I'm describing can only occur in an atmosphere of complete acceptance.

How can that mood be achieved if a wife hears comments like "Is that all you did with your day—take care of the kids?" "Why don't you exercise more," "I can't believe you thought we needed to buy that," or "Why can't you look more like that new woman at church?" How can a wife feel emotionally connected and cherished if she believes her husband sees her as stupid? How can she be naked and unashamed if she feels criticized every time she takes her clothes off? Even more, how emotionally close can a woman feel to a husband who walks through life with his eyes at breast level—especially at the level of other women's breasts? The answer to that last question is "not very."

If HD is a problem for women, then husbands have their own condition to contend with. I call it CWM. No, it's not Country Western Music. It is a Critical Wife or Mom. In giving this condition an acronym, I'm not making light of the problem. A man may be able to function physically when it comes to sex, but without the complete acceptance of a loving wife, sex for him becomes more of a power play than a celebration of intimacy. However, that lack of acceptance can certainly affect physical performance as well. Although an accurate statistic is not available, sex therapists agree that a huge percentage of male erectile difficulties are due to either performance anxiety or the criticism that comes from a significant female in his life.

If a husband's earning power is constantly demeaned, if he feels nagged about not doing enough with the kids, or if he is ridiculed because he's not handy when it comes to household repairs, he can never truly be intimate with his wife. If he feels like a failure because his wife never seems satisfied, he'll enter into the sexual relationship feeling a great deal of shame. If his wife often speaks admiringly of other men but never of him, or if she continually communicates disappointment with any part of his life, especially his sexual performance, he won't experience true sexual intimacy.

In the last chapter, we discussed the power of orgasm in intimacy and looked at how that power is most intensely felt when we are able to release control to our mates and allow ourselves to be completely vulnerable. That vulnerability and loss of control is only fully realized in the gift of being completely naked and completely unashamed. It is in that state of being truly and fully exposed to our mates that God has created the conditions where sexual pleasure reaches its sacred pinnacle. It is in giving ourselves to one who accepts us wholly that we most reflect what God intended to be holy: sensual sexual intimacy shared between a husband and a wife.

Finally, after first standing naked and unashamed before God by the gift of His grace and then after giving the gift of acceptance to our mates, we must take one other risk. We must be willing to trust the one we love. Despite what all previous experiences have taught us, we must risk revealing the things we've fought so hard to hide. It's only by our mates knowing and loving us regardless of our failures that we can find a release from shame. It's always a tremendous breakthrough in marital therapy when the long-hidden secrets finally find daylight and a counselor can say, "Well, look at that. Your mate learned something that you've worked so hard to keep hidden, and he's still sitting here. He didn't disappear." That moment almost always marks a breakthrough in sexual fulfillment as well. When it comes to sexual intimacy, the process of risk and trust is a continuous circle.

MAKING A CHOICE

You may wonder how you can break down the barriers after years of not fully accepting each other. You may feel that you've shown a lack of acceptance for so long that the damage may never be undone. How can you two go from being loaded down with shame to standing naked before each other and being completely unashamed? Surprisingly, you get there the very same way you got married in the first place.

Over the years I have rappelled off cliffs, explored underwater caverns, fought in martial arts tournaments, and even jumped out of a plane (wearing a parachute, of course). But none of that wackiness has ever been as nerve-wracking as being engaged to Amy. I don't mean the part about asking her to marry me. I'm recalling the six-month roller-coaster experience that followed my innocent proposal of marriage.

Being married to Amy was the one thing I wanted more than anything in life. So what was the matter? In my most honest moments, I admitted that I was afraid of first being found lacking and then being rejected. I was marrying way out of my league (like most guys I know). Amy was a godly, beautiful woman. I should have been on my knees thanking God for her, but I was lying awake at night worried that I'd be exposed for who I really was. I was deathly afraid that during our six months of preparing to walk down the aisle, Amy would find out something about me that would convince her not to marry me.

Imagine my relief on that July afternoon when my stunning bride emerged from the back doors of the sanctuary smiling right at me! How could this be happening? She certainly wasn't desperate; she'd had plenty of other opportunities. She wasn't deceived; she was fully aware of many of my faults and failures. So why was she still walking toward me, willing to live her life with me in the "blessed estate of marriage"? Why didn't someone with good sense stand up and yell, "Run, girl, run!" The answer to why she was walking down that aisle to me is very simple and yet powerful enough to change the world: She chose to.

We exercise unbelievable power whenever we make a choice. By far, one of the most fulfilling events in human experience is being freely chosen by someone to be that person's husband or wife. More powerful still is when we, as mates, continue to choose to love and accept one another on a daily basis. Love remains a choice, it is a decision, it is something we make up our minds to do. And accepting my spouse, even, as C. S. Lewis says, if she is a "beggar woman who never learns to wash behind her ears,"[7] is something I can and must make up my mind to do.

Through our free will, my spouse and I can decide to break down the barriers that have built up between us. We can reverse the habit of lack of acceptance. We can overcome our shame by choosing the things that elevate acceptance and defeat shame. The choice of acceptance is the best present any groom could ever give his bride. It's the one Adam gave to Eve. And it's the same gift God calls us to give to our spouse today. For it's only in the state of being naked and unashamed that we can enter the Promised Land of holy sex.

To be naked and completely unashamed means to stand before your mate and say, "Here's my body. Here are my emotions. Here are my thoughts about God. Here is my history with all of my hopes, my fears, my dreams, my failures. I stand here naked—physically, emotionally, and spiritually. Here are all the things that I've tried to keep hidden. But standing before you, I feel loved, accepted, and cherished." I'm not suggesting that you confess every bad thing you've ever done and every bad thought you've ever had. But you should give your mate the gift that will ultimately set both of you free: the gift of accepting one another, no strings attached. You also need to give each other the gift of your full self, completely trusting that your mate will accept what goes on inside you and by genuinely caring about what goes on inside of your spouse.

When we choose to accept our mates and thereby become an agent to free them from their shame, we must handle with utmost care the things we learn. It's all too common for people to share a weakness or a hurt, only to have it thrown back in their face during the next argument. Consider the woman who shares with her partner that she is insecure because of her critical father. Then, when she asks her husband not to go out with the boys this weekend, a fight ensues, and the husband says, "You don't want me to go because you're insecure!" Loving your spouse means choosing not to fight using intimate personal revelations as weapons.

The Power of Choosing Again

When I was in college I often had lunch with a friend who was married. It wasn't unusual for him to comment on the appearance of women who walked by. "Bubba," I'd say, "you're a married man. What are you doing looking at other women?" His response: "Just because I'm on a steady diet doesn't mean I can't look at the menu." Six years later I got married, and I learned a critical lesson: The menu is closed!

I have another friend who didn't marry until he hit his midthirties. He used to tell me that one of the things that scared him about getting married was that he was going to have to give up all of the other potential marriage candidates. Using my counselor voice, I would answer that concern with "You're dang right you will!" When I chose to marry Amy, I chose to give up every other woman in the world. I chose to accept her as God's exclusive gift to me. I chose to let her be the only one with whom I would share all sexual intimacy. That includes intimacy of the eyes, intimacy of the mind, intimacy of my memories, and intimacy of my imagination. When I look at a woman, it has to be Amy. When I think about a woman, it has to be Amy. When I fantasize about a woman, it can be none other than Amy. Those are choices I make gladly and have never regretted.

I'm not saying that I've been able to avoid all lustful thoughts. I can say, however, that as part of the process of being naked and unashamed, Amy is my ally in the battle against all that may attack our intimacy. She prays for me, she challenges me, and she throws away—at my request—the *Sports Illustrated* swimsuit issue before I ever see that day's mail. She is my ally to fulfill Paul's challenge to "take captive every thought to make it obedient to Christ" (2 Corinthians 10:5).

There's an old country song with a chorus that speaks a great truth that all women would love to hear. Talking to a wife of many years, singer Randy Travis asserts that if he had it to do all over again, even considering all the other women in the world, he'd choose no woman but his wife.

Such acceptance is a gift, and it is a choice. God has given our mate as a gift. So gladly accept, every day, the gift of your mate as he or she is. And choose him or her again tomorrow. Then, the next day, make the same choice again.

Let the naked-and-unashamed experience—the one that is best expressed as "Whoaaa! Man!"—begin!

QUESTIONS FOR CONVERSATION

1. Have you ever been in a situation, even dating back to childhood, in which you were made to feel ashamed of your body? Has anyone ever walked in on you while you were getting

dressed? In either case, share with your spouse the experience and the related feelings. How did that and similar experiences affect how you feel about yourself today?

2. After reading this chapter, what does being naked and unashamed mean to you? Share with each other your definitions and expectations of living together in a naked-and-unashamed relationship.

3. What conditions in your relationship work against the naked-and-unashamed experience? What areas of your marriage, other than sex, do you feel lack intimacy? Set some clear and specific goals for overcoming those barriers.

4. Have you fully dealt with the shame issues in your life? If not, share with your mate how he or she can help you overcome these. If necessary, make the commitment to seek competent outside help that can, by God's grace, lead you through the healing process.

5. Before answering this question, commit your time together to God in prayer. Then lovingly and honestly share with each other how you feel your mate's behavior is adding shame to your life. How and when do you feel a lack of acceptance? Prayerfully commit to creating the atmosphere of naked and unashamed that you both need and desire.

Chapter 5

Meta-Sex

Why All of Life Affects Sexual Intimacy

> If marriage were only bed, we could have made it.
>
> —MARILYN MONROE
> (on her failed marriage to Joe DiMaggio)

For those of you who read the table of contents, thought the title of this chapter was *mega*-sex, and turned here first, welcome. I hope you're not too discouraged now that you realize the topic is actually *meta*-sex. But before you return this book to the shelf, let me share something with you. If you truly desire mega-sex, defined as a fulfilling, soul-touching experience, you first need to understand the life-transforming experience of meta-sex. Without it, you'll never satisfy the longing for a truly meaningful and lasting sexual encounter.

Meta-sex involves viewing your sexual relationship in the context of the rest of your life. Your love life isn't a periodic, isolated event that stands apart from your work, your parenting, your finances, or even your in-laws. We aren't designed to be creatures who can divorce one segment of life from another. Under the surface, we're a network of interconnected parts. We're whole beings, which means that a force exerted on one part of our lives will cause movement in other areas. A stressful day at work can bring on a headache, and stress at home can make us less productive at work. Worry over our appearance or anxiety stemming from a mistake we've made can affect everything from our sleep to our disposition to what we eat to how much money we spend. The various parts of our lives are interconnected, and this interconnection is especially key to our sex lives.

Now, for what meta-sex is not. It's not about prolonging orgasm, increasing frequency, or enhancing sex through daring experimentation. As a matter of fact, meta-sex has very little to do with the act of sex. Instead, it focuses on the effect of everything—and I mean *everything*—that surrounds the act of sex.

I first thought of the term *meta-sex* as I was reading about meta-communication theories. These theories hold that before we can learn to communicate well, we must first understand *why* we communicate. We need to discern what we think about communicating and how everything that happens in our world—both past and present—affects how we speak and how we listen. It's imperative to realize how these and other factors, many of which we're unaware of, influence our ability to communicate.

For the sake of this discussion, then, let's think of sex as a form of communication. Indeed, it's the deepest, most intimate form of physical, emotional, and spiritual communication. Praying openly with one another would be the only interaction more intimate on the emotional and spiritual levels, though praying lacks the same physical depth. Sex connects all three realms.

The faithful practice of meta-sex will deepen our physical intimacy. So as we've given our mates the gift of acceptance, we must now give our marriages the gift of coupling. The process of coupling, often a term used to designate the sexual act itself, creates the context that's needed for sex to become not only all that God intends, but everything that we hope for as well.

A Truck, a Talk, and the Truth

When Amy and I got married, the only financial debt that she brought into our new life together was an auto loan. I, on the other hand, owed money on my truck, a student loan, a current school bill, and, oh, maybe a credit card or two. This was something virtually unheard of in my wife's world. As far as Amy was concerned, you simply didn't spend money if you didn't have it. I took the view that you had to spend money to make money—or at least to have fun.

Our expectations couldn't have been farther apart. Amy was looking forward to getting married, starting a great sex life, creating and following a budget, and continuing to live frugally. I was looking forward to getting married and starting a great sex life. I figured the other stuff would work itself out somehow.

We got married and, through fits and failures and more and more successes, we did arrive at what we thought was a great sex life. But we never seemed to get it together financially. When Amy would ask me about creating a budget, I'd say, "Yeah, we need to get to that. But hey, want to hear something I just read about sex?" Finally, in what I call a pots-and-pans experience (it gets your attention like someone banging on—or throwing—pots and pans), my patient bride said, "I wish you cared as much about our finances as you do about our sex life."

Bam! It hadn't sunk in until then.

Amy cared enough about me and about our marriage not to give up on an issue that was critical to our marital intimacy. She knew that if we continued to follow the financial course we were on, trouble loomed. My wife also knew something else that I'd been ignoring: My lack of concern about something that was important to her was beginning to affect her ability to give herself to me completely. Our financial habits truly were a meta-sex issue.

THE FOUR PHASES OF META-SEX

To picture the four phases of meta-sex, imagine a baseball diamond with first, second, and third base plus home plate. These four bases form the foundation of the meta-sex experience. Just as in baseball, each base must be touched if you hope to make it home.

Getting to first base means learning that sex is a holy, mysterious, and worshipful celebration created by a loving God. It's knowing that sex is God's way of introducing the transcendent into the earthly, specifically in the entwining of the bodies of two human beings who are committed to each other in marriage and who offered each other the gift of total acceptance. Nothing else in your sex life will fall into place without understanding and accepting the holiness of marital sex.

That said, let's head for second base. We arrive there when we realize the truth behind what my wife drilled into my thick head early in our marriage. Whether it's out-of-control finances, emotional distance, parenting issues, or something else that needs attention, if you don't take appropriate action, that neglect will adversely affect your sex life. No couple can enjoy a mutually fulfilling sexual connection if other significant issues are being ignored.

Although the issues surrounding sex often differ for husbands and wives, both women and men want and need to feel loved; we want to feel that we matter to someone else. And we'll never feel that we matter deeply to another human being if our mate is nonchalant about things that matter to us. When we accept that truth, we've reached second base.

When it comes to meta-sex, we don't get to second base by unbuttoning a blouse. (We'll leave that definition in the high-school locker room.) We get to second base by opening our eyes and our ears so we'll know what matters to our mates. Dr. Vernon Grounds, one of my original mentors and a pioneer in the field of Christian counseling, used to say that a good definition of love is simply this: What matters to you, matters to me; what happens to you, matters to me. Armed with that perspective, we go on to show our love through our actions. We show with our actions that our spouse and his or her concerns, passions, life events, and hurts matter to us. After all, how can we fully give ourselves to naked-and-unashamed sexuality if we feel that our partner doesn't care about the things that matter to us? If significant issues are left unattended, we can't experience the fullness of holy sex.

As a Spouse Thinketh

Before reaching third base, you must examine *how* you think about sex and *what* you think of it. It might not occur to you that something a spinster aunt or even a preacher said long ago about the unseemliness of sex actually left a lasting impression on you. You may still hear a voice screaming that sex is not supposed to be "good," that it's wrong to enjoy sex.

Or you might not realize how your early expectations of sex still affect you. Think back to high school when guys were telling tales of incredible backseat exploits (heavily embellished, no doubt). Even many years later, those stories may leave you feeling unsatisfied with your partner's responsiveness. Or if your view of how sex is "supposed to be" is founded on romance novels or almost any aspect of the visual entertainment world, you may not realize how much you are focusing on performance, a perfect body, and orgasm.

Amid a series of warnings about cheating, lusting after wealth, and selfishness, King Solomon wrote the familiar proverb: "For as he thinketh in his heart, so is he" (Proverbs 23:7, KJV). Similarly, the New Testament is full of exhortations to think about the things that lead to Christlike behavior and produce fruit that honor Him. Paul writes, "Finally, brothers, whatever is true, whatever is noble, whatever is right, whatever is pure, whatever is lovely, whatever is admirable—if anything is excellent or praiseworthy—think about such things" (Philippians 4:8; see also Colossians 3:2). The

Greek word for *think* in this verse is *logizesthe,* which means "to reckon, consider, calculate, or count as true." It is the same word used in Romans 6 when we are told to count ourselves dead to sin and in James when Abraham's faith is said to be "credited to him as righteousness" (2:23). The word carries with it the idea that we don't just let our minds roam freely, thinking about whatever pops into our heads. Instead, we direct our thinking toward something that is absolutely true. If we allow ourselves to think about sinful behaviors or ideas and assumptions that are untrue or immoral, those influences will define what we will become.

To some degree, we're all affected by wrong thinking when it comes to sex. However, we don't have to be addicted to pornography or obsessed with seduction fantasies for our sexual lives to be robbed of the pleasure that God intends for us. We can forfeit that pleasure simply by thinking "seemingly" harmless thoughts that happen to be dead wrong.

A good example is what one of my old bosses used to call "stinkin' thinkin'"—negative thoughts such as "That'll never work" and "I could never accomplish that." Negative, self-defeating thinking will keep you from achieving what is best in life. Dwelling on failure in your mind usually leads to actual failure in your life. Stinkin' thinkin' affects couples who believe that meaningful and fulfilling sex lives apply only to the "beautiful people" or to "people who haven't suffered as I have." "I could never have a great sex life. I guess I just don't deserve it"—That's stinkin' thinkin', and you need to identify it and rid it from your mind.

THE SEXUAL WOMAN

Let me tell you the story of Jake and Karen. This account is not the experience of just one Jake and Karen, however, but that of hundreds of couples just like them. Karen is between the age of twenty-five and forty-five, is married, and has one or more children (age twelve and under). Karen is outgoing, energetic, active in her church, and has too many friends to count.

Her husband, Jake, is a caring man and has achieved significant success in his career. He often tells Karen how attractive she is. He's a good father and willingly pitches in around the house. He puts the kids to bed as often as Karen does. With so much going for them, what's there to complain about? Well, really only one thing. The only marital issue Karen complains about is sex.

It's not that Karen doesn't like sex. She is, for the most part, orgasmic, and she has memories of regularly enjoying sex during the first year or two of marriage. Her main issue now is simply that she doesn't desire intercourse very often. In counseling, when she mentions how often she and Jake have sex, her estimate greatly exceeds the number that Jake remembers. (At this point, some "Jakes" usually want to pull out a calendar that shows the paltry few times they've "done it." Bad move, Jake.)

Many therapists and doctors would diagnose Karen's symptoms as inhibited sexual desire and identify the cause as a hormone imbalance. Birth control pills, antidepressants, or other medications can certainly affect a woman's hormonal balance. However, there's a growing movement that wants to treat all women with low sexual desire as having hormone problems. A common treatment involves giving women testosterone injections, which have considerable side effects for many women. Furthermore, the use of testosterone and the results are controversial at best.

Some women may very well need hormone treatments. For many women like Karen, however, hormones aren't the problem, and past sexual trauma, although an issue for many women, isn't an issue for Karen. For her and the multitudes of women like her, the problem is her sexual paradigm: her view of what a sexual woman is. The obstacle she can't overcome is simply that her definition of who she is doesn't include "a woman who deeply desires and enjoys sex."

Karen sees herself as a follower of Christ, a mother, a faithful wife, and someone who is trying to fulfill the lofty standards set forth in Proverbs 31.

The woman described there is accomplished, disciplined, and competent; she knows where she's headed and how she's going to get there. This picture is widely regarded as defining the successful Christian woman. But since the passage doesn't include any mention of sex, much less any mention of a woman who desires sex and enjoys it regularly, a woman's sexuality is often omitted from the Christian ideal.

During an early counseling session, I asked Karen to describe her image of a woman who thoroughly enjoys sex, is "a little wild" in bed, and occasionally initiates sex. She described that sort of woman as "single, loose, immoral, a seductress" and added that such a woman would be "provocatively dressed." Karen might have been describing that divorced woman who's been on the prowl at Jake's office.

My response to Karen surprised her. "Actually, the woman I was describing is a married, middle-aged mom who's a committed follower of Christ."

"That can't be," Karen told me. "It doesn't fit."

Consider, though, some of the many reasons why Karen's original description of herself didn't include a woman who fully enjoys sex. First, she and Jake are teaching their children to live sexually moral lives in a world where sex can kill you. Also, since the world takes sex so lightly and demeans it in every way imaginable, Karen finds it hard to see herself as someone who can be sexually uninhibited. Furthermore, the fact that she has gone through some of the physical and mental changes associated with motherhood creates a conflicting picture: "I'm a mother; I can't be sexy."

Another major contributor to Karen's original paradigm is the typical view her friends have of sex. "I don't know one person whom I would consider a godly woman who enjoys sex like you're talking about," Karen said.

"I do," I replied. Over the following weeks of counseling, we developed a new picture that added "sexual" to the image of a committed Christian woman. By processing much of what is discussed in this book, Karen and Jake were able to see that being a woman who deeply desired and enjoyed sexual intimacy was not contradictory to being a devoted wife, mother, and follower of Christ. Keeping this new and healthy image in mind is one way a woman enters into the fullness of holy sex.

In the book *Intimate Issues,* Linda Dillow and Lorraine Pintus ask this question: "How can American women change their [sexual] mind-set from boring to sizzling? By continuing to seek God's perspective on sex, a perspective that does not change or vary from culture to culture. God urges, 'Eat, friends; drink and imbibe deeply, O lovers' (Song of Solomon 5:1, NASB)."[1]

Women and men alike need to grasp the truth that God is pleased when His children enjoy His gift of sex within the boundaries of marriage. I asked Karen if she'd be surprised to know that God smiles when His children (including women) enthusiastically give themselves to holy sexual pleasure. She didn't answer. But as we studied the passions and joys of the lovers in the Song of Songs, Karen began to understand the changes she needed to consider.

THE SIN OF NEGATIVITY

The tendency of Christian women to view themselves as sexually sedate beings is only one barrier to holy sex. Consider now another.

All of us, men and women alike, are affected by what we let our minds dwell on. If our mental representation of who is having "great sex" stems from romance novels, movies, or soap operas, we'll be handicapped by a warped view. If we allow our minds to dwell on jokes, magazine surveys, or water-cooler conversations that deal with sex as an impersonal physical experience, we'll never seek the oneness nor experience the freedom that sexual intimacy was designed to provide. If we use our brainpower to form a critical picture of our spouses, our marriages, or our mating practices, we are, in fact, violating the sanctity of our God-created oneness. And we are robbing our mates and ourselves of the grace of holy sex.

On occasion, my wife finds herself in a group of women when a lively game of Bash the Husbands begins. Amy has no desire to play the game, so she tries to redirect the conversation or she simply excuses herself. She doesn't do this because she's married to the perfect man. If she joined the bashing game, she'd probably come out the state champion. She avoids the game for two very simple, yet powerful, reasons. One, she and I have made a commitment that, if we have a problem with each other, we'll tell only one person: each other. Two, we both realize the truth of the old proverb: "A marriage is only as good as it is in public." In other words, deal with your problems at home, not in front of friends.

And we must guard our unspoken words as well: We must keep our thoughts about our mates pure. Concentrating on pure thoughts doesn't mean ignoring problems. Our thoughts are pure when we see our mates and their bodies as they truly are: God's gift to us. We don't bash our spouse when we're talking to friends, and we don't secretly wish they were someone else. Likewise, we keep our thoughts about sex pure. Not pure from a staid, inhibited, or "sex as duty" sense, but pure in that we savor the fact that the God of the universe smiles when His children "imbibe deeply."

CATCH THE FOXES

Song of Songs 2:15 is a strange verse about catching "the foxes, the little foxes that ruin the vineyards." Both counselor and marital researcher Scott Stanley[2] and psychologist John Trent[3] have concluded that these "foxes" are the little things in a marriage that, if left unchecked, will eventually undermine the relationship, just as foxes will destroy a vineyard. In marriage, for instance, the little foxes can be mishandled conflict that is allowed to fester until it results in barriers between spouses. And when it comes to the gift of our sexual connection, we must catch and destroy the little foxes that run through our thoughts and threaten to kill the passion and fun God desires for us.

So what does your mind tend to dwell on when sex is a topic? *I'd enjoy having sex with my husband if he were more like Mary's husband* or *Sex would be better if my wife would just lose a few pounds.* Or perhaps you find yourself thinking, *I need to come up with a good reason to avoid sex tonight* or *I need to figure out how I can talk my frigid mate into having sex tonight.* When you allow thoughts that are critical or demeaning, no matter how slight, to fill your head, they will kill your passion. We need to catch those foxes, get them out of our minds, and then work hard in the vineyard to keep passion blooming.

Other thoughts about our mate and sex, however, need to be dealt with differently. If a husband or a wife is turned off to sexual intimacy due to certain behaviors that can be changed, then those behavior changes need to be dealt with in love. If innuendos or comments, ways of touching or responding, or even elements of hygiene cause you to think negatively about your sexual relationship, then lovingly address those issues. All little foxes need to be chased away through prayer and open, accepting conversation.

THE ENVIRONMENT OF PASSION

Now think about the moment you fell in love with your mate. Did you suddenly find yourself overwhelmed with attraction, or did the feeling emerge gradually after your lover had been courting you for a while? (Don't kid yourself. Women do a lot of courting too.) Did you *grow into love* after your girlfriend or boyfriend had done hundreds of little things that made you feel special? For most of us, love came after demonstrations of care, after our partner learned our likes and dislikes, and after he or she took the time to pay attention to the details of life that are important to us.

I don't believe we fall in love. Instead, I'm convinced that we grow into love over time as we each create an atmosphere of kindness and care and mutual interest. We show each other that we are valued, that we are sought after, that we are cherished. Thus, the early passion of a relationship doesn't just happen. It comes as a result of the atmosphere that we both create.

The same is true of the passion that exists throughout the years of marriage. It's not destined to die out, as our culture would lead us to believe. Quite the opposite: It should continue to grow more intense the longer we are together. Marital passion is created by a husband and wife who continue to practice those courtship skills that were so irresistible when they first grew to love each other. In marriage, those skills include sexual intimacy, which plays a major role in the creation, celebration, and sustaining of our passion.

In commenting on passion, Dillow and Pintus write, "We agree that it's difficult to keep the passion burning, but not impossible. Sex isn't an event. It is an environment. We must make passion a priority and then set an atmosphere where passion can reign."[4] They also connect a woman's identity to the passion level in her marriage. "Recapturing passion has first to do with your attitude about being a lover to your husband. Passion begins with priorities, not genitals."[5]

The same holds true for men. If you want to feel more passion for your wife, and you wish she would show more passion for you, then you have to make it a priority. We don't "fall in passion" any more than we "fall in love." The passion happens as a result of loving actions. I'm not advocating a manipulative or insincere display of affection for the purpose of increasing one's chances of having sex. Spouses need a consistent, sincere habit of caring for each other. The cherishing behaviors promised on the wedding day lead to intimacy that strengthens a marriage. These cherishing behaviors also lead to a more fulfilling sex life for both a husband and a wife.

HEADING TOWARD HOME

Tagging third base helped us build physical intimacy in five ways. We identified the past influences that continue to affect our attitudes and expectations regarding sex; we learned to see ourselves as sexual beings, even as sexy beings; and we learned to banish self-defeating thought patterns. In addition, we focused on true and pure thoughts about our mates and our sexual relationship, and we saw how to establish a long-term environment that keeps passion growing. Now that we've rounded third base, we can head for home. But first, let's pause for a quick quiz.

It's 5:30 P.M. on a weeknight, and the Hour of Anarchy has begun. Mom just got home from running errands with kids in tow, and she's digging through the freezer to see what tonight's dinner is going to be. Johnny is hollering from upstairs, wanting Mom to tell him where he left his baseball cleats. Teenager Mindi has made it to the dining room table after climbing over piles of backpacks, coats, and shoes, blind to the benefit of putting everything where it belongs. She's doing her homework with the stereo blaring (but not so loudly that she can't shout, "What's the capital of North Dakota?"). Little Billy is "helping" Mom by pulling canned vegetables out of the cabinet and piling them on the floor while singing loudly along with Mindi's music.

The phone rings repeatedly (either for Mindi or whoever needs siding, windows, or a new mortgage). Neighbor kids (who apparently don't do homework) are knocking at the door wanting to play. And, oh, there's the small matter of no one remembering to let the dog out. Is that a wet spot on the carpet?

At 5:50 P.M., the garage door opener is heard, and soon Dad walks in. Now for the test question: What should Dad do first?

1. Say, "Hi," ask where the mail is, and flip on the television news.

2. Ask, "When's dinner?" Then add, "Remember I've got a church league basketball game tonight."

3. Remember that he's supposed to tell his wife all about his day, so he immediately launches into a detailed description of just how frustrating today was because the office copier broke down and Sid took credit for landing the big contract that he actually had nothing to do with and...

4. Give his wife a quick hug and kiss, pick up Billy and put the canned goods back into the cabinet, help Mindi with her homework (while turning down the stereo), find Johnny's baseball cleats, let the dog out, and as he heads out to the backyard with Billy, holler back, "Hon, I'm gonna skip the basketball game tonight so I can run Johnny to practice. When I get back, I'll put Billy to bed."

Okay, the quiz is easy because you know how you're *supposed* to answer. The real question is "How often do you or I actually live out answer number four?" In other words, "What do I do to show my mate that he or she matters to me—that he or she is my priority—every moment of the day?"

Throughout the day and evening, until our heads hit the pillow at night, our goal as wives and husbands should be to communicate to our mates how much they matter to us. Does that mean we can't play in a basketball league, read the mail, or have other separate activities? Of course not. But those activities, in and of themselves, usually aren't the problem. Typically, the problem is the overall message that we communicate. It's what we communicate at the meta-level.

Every marriage counselor knows many men who have flunked the above test; they all have a story of a husband who comes home, goes straight to the mail and flips on the television news, grunts through dinner, opens his briefcase to catch up on some work, makes a few phone calls, and watches more television. Then he goes to bed and within seconds reaches out to stroke his wife's breast, convinced that that's all it takes to "get her in the mood." Quick clue: It isn't.

Because of the overabundance of scenarios like this, most Christian marital therapists and researchers are quick to hammer home a man's need to be more understanding of his wife, to open up emotionally to her, and to overall be more communicative. Even without my wife joining the Husband Bashing Game, many (including myself) are quick to point out the many ways men fall short when it comes to loving their wives sexually in a God-honoring, sacred way. However, it seems we are also hesitant to challenge the women to grow and stretch. But as in meta-communication, meta-sex is very much a two-way street.

Just as many men fail to understand how important it is to become deeply involved in all emotional aspects of his wife's world, many women fail to understand how deeply sex can be connected to emotional oneness for their husbands. Part of this is due to the fact that many men do a very poor job articulating the incredibly intense and immense sensations that are occurring within them far beyond what is happening on the physiological level. To many men, being one sexually is *the* place where they feel most one—most naked and unashamed—with their mates. However, if they are unable to fully communicate that to their wives, their desire for sex can come across as just that: a desire for *sex*.

Therefore, it is not only important for husbands to attempt to express what they truly feel about their sexual connection with their wives, but it is equally important for wives to know that, even in the absence of a meticulous exhaustive explanation of the sexual insides of their mates, much of their husband's desire for sex truly is a desire for oneness, a oneness that brings comfort and security in our harried world and helps them feel loved. As such, women would do well to respond more positively and more openly to what their husbands are seeking. No, I am not saying wives should therefore have sex whenever and in whatever way their husbands want. As the rest of the book testifies, that would not be holy sex. However, as we will discuss in the next chapter, wives need to know and accept that although there are many ways the sexual experience is similar for both wives and husbands, there are many ways that it is different. Understanding that is key to understanding meta-sex.

For both husbands and wives, meta-sex is the realization that the more we communicate through our words and actions that our mates are the ones we value and treasure above all as God's perfect gift, the more we'll experience passion. Constant loving words and behaviors lead to anticipation, one of the greatest igniters of the fires of passion. Sex is a wonderful experience when we longingly desire to be with the person long before we are. And it is the meta-sex encounters of a twenty-four-hour-a-day relationship that creates those wonderful anticipatory feelings. That's how you get to home plate.

THE ELEPHANT IN THE BEDROOM

Whenever a couple with an undiscussed "predominant presenting problem" (an outward symptom such as alcoholism or sexual infidelity) comes in to see me, we usually begin with a few minutes of informal "let's get comfortable" conversation. Then I broach the subject by saying, "Okay, let's talk about the elephant standing in the room." We all know it's there, although the clients have been working hard to avoid it.

For many couples, sex is the same way. It's an obvious, sometimes deeply troubling part of their marriage, but they still want to avoid dealing with it. They hide behind excuses: "Talking about sex just isn't me" or "I'll be fine without dealing with it." That is not, however, a choice that we as Christians have. If we desire a marriage that honors God and fulfills His design for oneness, we can't ignore our sex life. Sexual intimacy wasn't designed to be something we fight about, it was not designed to be taken for granted or abused, and it was not designed to be disregarded when we become uncomfortable talking about it. If we are to be obedient to God, then we must keep our marriage bed "undefiled" (Hebrews 13:4, KJV). And that covers a lot more than simply not having an affair or not lusting after a person other than our mate. Keeping our marriage bed pure is also about keeping our sexual relationship a place of mutually desired celebration. No matter how difficult or unsettling a sexual issue is, we need to deal with it. If necessary, we need to seek the help of a pastor or a qualified Christian counselor or therapist.

How to Become Meta-Sexy

In baseball, a suicide squeeze play is sometimes attempted when there's a runner on third base and your team desperately needs to score a run. As the pitcher begins his windup, the runner takes off for home. It's the job of the batter to bunt the ball into the field of play. The batter will most likely be thrown out at first base, hence the nickname "suicide," but his goal was not to get safely on base, but to "squeeze" the runner home. Sounds easy, but it's hard to do in the big leagues. It's always a risk.

Getting to home in meta-sex is perilous as well. You may be considering a paradigm shift from status-quo sex to meta-sex, but you fear that it's way too risky. Your reluctance is understandable, but God's grace and power call us to rise above our fears. Love is an attitude and a series of actions that lead to passion. Since actions are choices, creating passion is a choice. It's a risk all of us who are married need to take, so where do we begin?

First, look at your prevailing attitude. Husbands, have you set yourself the goal of serving your wife, making her feel loved, valued, and cherished—24/7/365? Do you serve her outside the bedroom, no strings attached, regardless of what happens that night? And wives, what about your attitude and your self-definition? Remember that "your sense of sensuousness begins in your mind before your husband enters the room. Thinking sexually is a frame of mind, a focus."[6] In this case, if being "loose" means having a sexy attitude, that's a good thing. Go for it!

Second, do you work hard to set the stage for passion? Men, put down the sports page, save the mail for later, turn off the television, and let the answering machine get the phone. Speak lovingly to your wife, make the things that matter most to her matter to you, and touch her affectionately—in a nonsexual manner. Wives, encourage your husbands, show them that you desire them, and make them a priority. Honor them, respect them, and speak passion to them.

That's how you become meta-sexy.

PASSIONATE COMMITMENTS

To close the chapter, I'd like to share a few commitments that Amy and I have made to keep passion alive in our marriage. These aren't stone tablets brought down from the mountain. They are simply things that work for us. They might provoke some thinking about the things that will work best for you.

At the beginning of this chapter, I mentioned coupling. Coupling is a mind-set. It's the realization that even though I'm an individual, I need to think "couple" in everything I choose to do. In a world of work, kids, and church, Amy and I are constantly making schedule decisions. We've committed to avoid any obligations that would impinge on couple or family time without first talking to each other. Coupling is simply having a married mind-set, knowing that all we do affects the other.

Next, early in our relationship, we committed to talking to each other every day, even when one of us is traveling. Other than a couple of spiritual renewal retreats that involved seclusion and one backpacking trip in the Rockies, we've kept that commitment.

Third, we've chosen to keep things that happen outside our relationship from inordinately affecting what happens inside our relationship. If I have a rough day at work, I consciously decide not to bring it home. That doesn't mean I don't share with Amy that it was a frustrating day. It just means that I don't let a crummy day cause a lousy evening. On my drive home from the office, I pass over a creek. This is a visual reminder to me to dump my problems from work into the stream so I can go home and answer a higher calling: serving my wife.

Finally, we've made a decision about our bedroom. As the authors of *Intimate Issues* point out, most couples' bedrooms are places where dirty clothes get sorted, books and magazines are stacked, and clutter accumulates. I've also found that many couples use their bedroom as the place for conflict resolution. None of those activities is conducive to passionate love.[7] I encourage couples to consider their bedrooms as places of honor, free from both clutter and conflict. Now, I know we don't all (Amy and me included) have spare rooms where we can stash all our extra stuff. But I do believe that most couples can work harder to keep their bedrooms uncluttered and that they can also find another place to discuss conflicts. (I prefer a setting where we can sit and look into each other's eyes; it also makes it easier to drink coffee.) All of this is about creating an atmosphere that protects intimacy and enhances and encourages passion. The bedroom should be a place where we both look forward to simply being together.

In his book *The Life You've Always Wanted,* pastor John Ortberg states that "every moment is potentially an opportunity to be guided by God into His way of living. Every moment is a chance to learn from Jesus how to live in the kingdom of God."[8] Amy and I were so challenged by this statement that we stuck it on our bathroom mirror. When I look at it, I think about another way to apply this principle: Every moment of every day is potentially an opportunity to show our mates that we love them and value them. Every moment is a chance to learn from Jesus how to love our mates in a more giving, more unselfish way. Every moment is an opportunity to create and share passion and oneness. In doing that, we are also learning to live in the kingdom of God.

Score one for your marriage. You just hit a home run.

QUESTIONS FOR CONVERSATION

1. What are some of the wrong-headed things you have thought about sex in the past? Thinking back to your childhood, adolescence, and possibly even more recently, let your spouse in on some of your "adventures" in sex education. (As you do this, be careful not to reveal anything that would be unnecessarily painful to your mate). While you're talking, share any current "stinkin' thinkin'" that is affecting your sexual intimacy.

2. Did the story of Jake and Karen strike a chord with you? If so, how? Share with each other how you view passion. Share how you feel God views passion.

3. Reread the pop quiz in the section: Heading Toward Home. Reword the descriptions of Mom, Dad, Mindi, Johnny, and Little Billy to fit your own family situation. Then recall a time when one or both of you failed the test. Now, in light of the principles of meta-sex, create a new scenario in which you both would pass the test with flying colors. Commit to living out this scenario within the week.

4. What are you going to do to become meta-sexy? In a spirit of acceptance and joy, share ways that you both could increase your intimacy in all other aspects of your marriage.

5. If you really want to take your marriage into the Promised Land, then write yourself a reminder of the John Ortberg truth quoted at the end of the chapter. Put it where you'll see it every day. Train yourself to recognize that every moment of every day is potentially an opportunity to show your mate how much you love and value him or her. Write down your commitment to develop this mind-set. Ask God to help you live it out.

Chapter 6

Women and Men

Letting Our Differences Set the Stage for an Amazing Sexual Bond

> Women need a reason to have sex; men just need
> a place.
>
> —BILLY CRYSTAL

They say that politics makes strange bedfellows. On many occasions I've listened to a politician passionately promote an issue, only to hear myself say piously, "How can anyone with a brain bigger than a walnut believe that? Where's my pen? I'm writing a letter!" Then a few weeks later, I can see this same politician promoting something I actually agree with. *Strange,* I'll think, *His brain must have grown. He's actually right about that.* When people with opposing views actually join together on anything, it does seem strange.

I find it interesting, though, that we use the word *bedfellows* to describe the situation of opposites actually getting together. The phrase that word appears in implies that, in normal situations, those occupying the same bed are like-minded. No way. If politics puts strangely different people in the same bed, then marriage not only puts strangers in the same bed, but strangers who don't even speak the same language.

What husband hasn't suffered a brain cramp while trying to sort out the vast emotional differences between himself and his wife? What wife hasn't felt as if her husband considers her some sort of sexual apparatus, valued more for certain body parts than for who she is?

Of course, some of our differences are truly exciting. What husband hasn't relished the excitement of beholding the wonder of God's creation known as woman? What wife hasn't felt the thrill of being the sole recipient of her man's intense affections? Men and women are different, but that is precisely what keeps all these sparks flying between us. The very differentness inherent in being male and female both pulls us toward each other and drives us to distraction. Why in heaven's name would God create us this way? Well, it's not some divine practical joke. I'm convinced that being opposite sets the stage for a sexual bond that exceeds our wildest imagination.

Before we wade into a discussion of the differences between men and women, let me introduce my best friend and the coauthor of this chapter. My wife, Amy, will join me as we explore the wonderful, challenging, God-designed differences between women and men.

A quick disclaimer: Amy and I are writing this chapter not as experts, but as fellow strugglers. We have much to learn about sex and would never pretend that we have it all together. And as we offer our perspectives and advice, we don't pretend that any of this is easy to practice. It's extremely difficult! But it is, we believe, the way that God intends husbands and wives to relate to each other.

WHY WE'RE SO DIFFERENT

Tim: Lewis Smedes, ethicist and professor emeritus at Fuller Theological Seminary, writes that it is our God-intended differences that cause women and men to be "driven toward each other until they again become 'one flesh' in intimate body-union."[1] Theologian Karl Barth believed that just as the full image of God is displayed on earth in male and female joined together, so too is the fullness of relational intimacy experienced in the differences between women and men.[2] Our distinctions were created so women and men could have an intimate relationship with each other in a way that uniquely complements and fulfills each of them.

As we examine these differences, we also will look at the disparities that many say exist but are not necessarily God-designed. Instead of reflecting true, God-instituted variances, much of the Mars and Venus drivel is simply an excuse to justify certain selfish behaviors. God calls us to serve one another, not to rationalize or whine.

Amy: Being a mom of two boys and a girl has taught me more than any book ever could about the innate differences between the sexes. Nobody taught my daughter to try on every woman's shoe she sees or to want to constantly visit the newborn babies in our cul-de-sac; and no one instructed my boys in the art of using a common stick as one hundred different weapons. This experience as a parent has reinforced for me the truth that it is God who created the differences between male and female. And marriage has taught me that these differences have very distinct purposes when it comes to intimacy. Our differences are not excuses to avoid doing something our mate may desire. God created Tim different from me so that he can meet my God-given needs—and I'm different from him so that I can meet his. Our heart's desire and struggle must be to do just that.

COMMON LIES ABOUT SEX

Tim: It's hard to live according to new ideas when old ideas are rooted so deeply inside us that they choke off any new growth. When it comes to the sexual experience of men and women, too many people hold on to a number of old, damaging lies.

Here's one of the biggest: Men *need* sex. (I'll continue as soon as the husbands' howls of protest die down.) Many men believe that they need sex to the same degree that they need food, water, and oxygen. I recently heard one historian explain why, prior to the 1950s, women were expected to be virgins until they were married, while it was fairly commonplace for unmarried men to visit brothels. The reason? It was accepted that men needed sex and women didn't.

On psychological theorist Abraham Maslow's hierarchy of needs pyramid, sex is listed at the base level of human survival, referring only to the need to procreate. Without sex, the race would die out (individuals themselves wouldn't die). Sex is not a survival need when it is sought for the sake of pleasure or physical release. Holy sexuality would actually show up at the top level on Maslow's chart under "self-actualization needs." Self-actualizing people are devoted to a cause outside themselves. As believers, we grow in our sexual experience as we move from an adolescent focus on what it does for me to a spiritual focus of how I can serve my mate.

Many men have approached their wives with the line, "Honey, it's been a few days. I really *need* to have sex." And many women grudgingly comply. The result is a sexual encounter that provides momentary physical pleasure for the husband while building sexual resentment in the wife. Not what I would call a holy experience. A great marriage does need great sex, but husbands don't need it to survive.

Amy: Even though a husband's survival doesn't depend on sex, for the most part men want sex more often than their wives do. Sociologists and anthropologists have tried to explain this discrepancy as an innate drive to propagate the species. A male needs to "plant his seed" as often as possible in order to guarantee the survival of the race. But that theory doesn't mesh with the theology of sex we have discussed; neither does it align with the typical male sexual experience. Even casual observation shows that a man on the prowl is not seeking to father more children; he is seeking personal pleasure. And from the Creator's perspective, sex is about oneness. So any motivation for sex among humans that doesn't have total oneness as its goal is selfishly motivated.

So why the gap in sexual desire between women and men? Why did God create us this way? Part of the answer is "He didn't." The great divide in sex drives has been created by something other than God. It's come because we've bought into the lie that a "normal" person wants sex all the time. Part of what men need to learn to do is temper their desire (this will be discussed in detail later), and part of what women need to do is realize that just as the frequently unholy state of sex does not come from God's plan, neither does the huge desire gap. Women also need to know that God created sex for their pleasure just as much as He did for men and that their sexual desires and responses are holy and sacred.

To know this biblically, we need only look to the Song of Songs, which paints a vivid picture of male and female sexual desire. We don't see a woman constantly being pursued by a man who desires sex more than she does. We don't see a woman who feels exploited, who is pressured into having sex. What we find is a passionate woman who strongly desires to be touched, kissed, and made love to. What a magnificent picture of the mutuality that God desires us to share.

So why don't more couples experience this mutual desire today? For many women, one reason is the lack of communication. A wife wants to feel connected to her husband. She needs to know that her husband is listening when she talks about the things that are important to her. A woman also wants to know what's going on in her husband's world. For a woman to enter into sex as a holy encounter, she needs to know her husband deeply.

On the other side of the bed, there is something very important for wives to discover: A husband's desire for sex with his wife is not always just about sex—it's often because he wants to feel loved.

Tim: Sex is never just sex. It's loaded with other meanings. If a marriage is void of intimacy, then sex is about power and escape. If a couple typically gets along well, then a man's desire to have sex with his wife usually means that he wants to feel loved and desired. Husbands often want their wives to initiate sex not so they can enact some adolescent fantasy, but because they want to feel that their wife desires them. That's why fights about sexual frequency often are really about the deeper, unspoken issue of a husband wanting to feel loved.

Amy: And that's why when a husband initiates sex and his wife casually says she's tired or not in the mood, her refusal is actually a big deal. Her husband is now feeling unloved and rejected. That's why communication is important. He needs to tell his wife how he is truly feeling. Sex involves strong emotions, a desire for a deep connection with your mate, and judgments about self-worth. Therefore, many women need to prayerfully examine their view of sex. Is it something you do merely to satisfy a physical urge of your husband and therefore you can say no, knowing he won't die and not worrying too much about it? Or is sexual intimacy a way for you to reach out and love your husband in way that touches him on a deeply emotional level and therefore makes him feel valued and loved? We wives must honestly decide if this is a way of reaching out and loving our husbands in which God wants us to grow.

Tim: Okay, let's say a guy is telling his wife what he's feeling, and his wife has learned that her husband enjoys feeling loved through their sexual relationship. Their sex life ought to just click into place; they'll both be perpetually fulfilled, right? Well, no. What we usually have is the battle of the "Me Firsts." Let me illustrate. I come home wanting to feel loved and cared for, and I have already used up my ten thousand words that social researchers say an average man speaks each day. Women, on other hand, average a whopping twenty-five thousand words per day (with gusts of up to seventy-five thousand). So not only have Amy and I been out of each other's world for eight-plus hours, but she has fifteen thousand words pent up inside ready to be unleashed! And after kids, homework, and other daily chaos, she wants to feel loved too.

Amy: I'm looking forward to Tim helping get the kids to bed and then sitting and having a quiet conversation as we share a cup of mocha coffee. (Have you picked up that we like coffee?) A back rub, a snuggle, a verbal reconnection, a resolution of a budget issue, and I can feel loved and ready for sleep.

Tim: I may be looking forward to getting the kids to bed, paying the bills, and asking about Amy's day while getting ready for bed. Afterward, I hope, we'll enjoy some sexual intimacy. Then I'll feel loved and ready to read until I go to sleep. (Let's see, a Clancy novel or a book on sexual theory?)

Amy: There's nothing wrong with either one of these scenarios. Tim and I speak on the phone at least once a day so we generally feel connected when the Hour of Anarchy hits, so it's not that I feel he's a stranger. It's simply that all I happen to want this particular evening is to talk. That's more than enough for me to feel loved.

Tim: And it's not that I feel Amy doesn't love me or doesn't enjoy making love. Neither is it that I don't take pleasure in our conversations. I enjoy the coffee and the conversation, but I still want the evening to end with some lovemaking. In other words, I want what I want. Like everyone else, I'm selfish.

STRIKING DOWN SELFISHNESS

Amy: Selfishness isn't limited to husbands. Wives are equally selfish, and therein lies the tension. Many times, it's easy to serve Tim by loving him sacrificially; at other times, it's very hard. Sometimes I even know I'm being selfish, but that knowledge doesn't always change my behavior. When I'm exhausted or worried or preoccupied with a big commitment coming up the next day, it's easy to rationalize that adding sex to the mix is just one thing too many. It can feel like just one more person wanting something from me.

Tim: Often just realizing our own selfishness is enough to change the way we react. We remember we're called to love one another by serving. So we must continue to work out our love for our mates, especially when the issue stems from our differences. There are times when I must be satisfied with Amy being satisfied. If all she needs is a neck massage and some catch-up conversation, that's what I need to provide. I must serve her by giving her what she needs.

If, for example, I come home and find Amy under attack from a clogged drain and the kids' school projects that are due tomorrow, I have a choice. I can either add to her pressure by suggesting she prepare for a little romance later that night, or I can put my sexual desires on hold, get out my plumbing tools, and call 1-800-SENDPIZZA to free up more home-work time. In other words, I can make it a priority to serve my wife instead of pouting.

Amy: Of course, serving each other's needs works both ways. But does serving mean that a wife has to comply every time her husband suggests they have sex? It's a common question, but not a particularly helpful way to word it. Having sex with your husband is not a "have to" situation. It's a "get to." Sex is a holy gift that a wife is privileged to give.

In the same way, just as sex is never just sex, declining an invitation to have sex should never be done with just a no. If a wife feels emotionally distant from her husband, she needs to tell him, "Honey, I'd love to be with you, but I need to know what's going on with you first. Can we sit and talk, or perhaps I could give you a back rub while we tell each other about our days." If it's a case of fatigue, the issue most frequently cited by women as a barrier to a better sex life,[3] a wife can say, "Babe, I'd love to be with you, but I really am tired tonight. Can we make plans to be together tomorrow night?" Be creative—and gentle. Remember that your goal is to communicate your desire to be intimate. Don't send a message that could be heard as rejection.

Speaking of fatigue, I feel God wants us to examine how it may be hurting or even destroying our sex life. Women, if you are frequently too tired to put any energy into a dynamic sex life with your husband, you must ask yourself, "Why is that?" Are you overcommitted? Do you have your kids overcommitted? Sex with your husband should not be the undone errand on your to-do list. You need to drop something else.

Husbands, is your wife fatigued all of the time because she feels like you are expecting her to take care of the house, the laundry, the cooking, the kids, *and* you? See what you can do for her on a regular basis to ease her fatigue. What can you do on a daily basis to make her life easier and help her feel refreshed, not exhausted. It's important to note that Jesus was not ever in a hurry or in a rush to get anywhere. He always had time for what is important. Sacred sex is important. We need to slow down and start taking better care of ourselves and each other.

TALKING ABOUT SEX

Tim: As we get better at expressing our feelings, appreciating each other, and increasing the emotional intimacy of our marriages, we also need to start talking about the sexual relationship itself. This is where both husbands and wives need to listen and learn.

Amy: A wife needs to tell her husband what she likes and doesn't like, including where she does and doesn't like to be touched and what she does and doesn't enjoy during sex. She needs to be able to say, "Stop," "Slow down," and "Touch me here." And she needs a husband who will respond without trying to change her.

As far as God is concerned, the only standard for sexual frequency and the only sexual preferences that matter are what the two of you want—assuming, of course, that your sexual activity falls within His boundaries of marriage, mutual consent, and no physical harm. Does this mean a woman doesn't ever try new things or stretch beyond her comfort zone? No. But she needs to know that her husband hears her, respects what he hears, and acts upon what he hears. She needs safe and open communication.

Tim: The best lover is not the husband who knows the best techniques; the best lover is the man who is the best student of his wife. Knowing what makes your mate uncomfortable and showing respect for those boundaries is key to your spouse being able to enjoy the freedom of being naked and unashamed. Likewise, a woman who acts purposefully in response to her husband's likes and desires—without violating her own convictions—is showing her mate how much she values him. We need to learn from each other.

Our culture says that being a great lover is something men should just know how to do. You think it's bad when a man gets lost and won't ask for directions? Just imagine what happens when a guy finds out he isn't meeting his wife's sexual needs! He won't just automatically pull over and ask for directions. But listen, guys. Being a great lover of your wife comes about as naturally as being an accomplished brain surgeon. It takes years of learning and dedication and, well, fun practice.

None of us is completely untainted by the world's false propaganda about sex. Even those who abstained from sex before marriage were still indoctrinated with the fantasy love stories of our culture that skewed our view of romance. And husbands, of course, heard their quota of locker-room tales of sexual conquest. Mostly lies, of course, but who knew that back then?

That's why we need to learn anew about sex. If each man and each woman sought to learn about sexual likes and dislikes only from their mates, we'd be free of almost all of our sexual conflicts. There would be no occasion for comparing practices, positions, preferences, or body shapes and sizes. We also need to learn from the Bible about God's design of holy sex—and about how it all works. But when it comes to what's enjoyable about sex, we need only one authority: our mates.

Amy: That is the essence of the holy sex experience: being strong enough to focus on our mate's needs above our own. There appears to be a contradiction here, I know. We're supposed to focus on our mate's needs and likes, and at the same time we're supposed to educate them about our own preferences. From the day we met until today, we are teaching our spouses about everything from our favorite foods to our taste in books, sports, and movies. We should teach them about our sexual feelings as well.

But where does that leave us when our mates teach us about a sexual preference that doesn't align with our own tastes? Though the depth of emotional commitment is certainly not the same, it can be similar to our choices for dining out. When I met Tim, I wasn't a big fan of Mexican food, and he wasn't real high on Chinese. This was a problem in light of the fact that Tim's family owned several Mexican restaurants. Well, over the years, we've both grown in our enjoyment of different foods. Tim will often bring home Chinese takeout, and I have become a Mexican food connoisseur. (I even love salsa on eggs.) The point is that we've both grown in culinary likes because we've both been willing to try new menus.

In sex, just as in food, we have likes and dislikes. But there are many areas in which we can discover a healthy resolution. Part of serving each other in the area of holy sex is finding that middle ground where we can come together and share an experience that meets each other's needs. But when we share our preferences, we don't then demand that our mate meet those needs. We leave the serving up to them. My job, as difficult as it may be sometimes, is to act on what Tim has taught me about his desires while continuing to grow and teach him about my own needs and preferences. Most wives, I believe, can grow in this area of serving their mates.

Tim: Men and women are both guilty of expecting their mates to read their minds. I'd rather have Amy just intuitively know what I'd prefer in the area of sex, but I have to admit that God didn't give her that ability. And I certainly can't read her mind either (and wives, that goes for your husband too). That's why we must teach our mates and why we must be willing to learn from them.

Having a conversation about your sexual likes and dislikes can be scary territory to venture into. A wife may need to express the hard truth that something her husband has been doing for years is actually a turnoff. Those things need to be shared. The bedroom is a place where our ego should not be on the line.

Amy: Experimenting with new techniques or positions or locations should be considered and even tried, but don't try every new thing all at once. If your husband suggests something that creates a serious conflict within you, share that with him. But if your mate is also doing everything he can to please you, then he won't force you to do anything that will cause you to feel used or demeaned. A husband who is serving his wife will never use lines like "If you love me, you'll do this…" Remember, love "is not self-seeking" (1 Corinthians 13:5). But if both spouses desire to give themselves to the other—even occasionally stepping outside their comfort zone—the relationship will continue growing and will remain exciting.

Tim: If you both choose to love and accept one another, your conversations about your sexual relationship will be some of your most intimate moments. As you learn to share what gives you the most pleasure and what makes you feel closer to each other, it will become much easier to regularly talk openly about your sex life. Getting started is the hardest part, so don't keep putting it off. Just like financial investments that benefit from compound interest, the sooner you start, the better the results. Set a time and venture out.

DIFFERENCES THAT MAKE SEX FUN

Amy: It's important to remember that men and women don't experience all aspects of sex the same way. Sorry, men, but most wives just aren't turned on by seeing their husbands in their underwear. It would be helpful for all of us to remember these gender-related differences and to accept what our mates tell us about their likes and dislikes.

When a woman tells her husband that she can enjoy intercourse without having an orgasm, he needs to accept that as truth. (I know most men go "Huh?" at that statement, but it's true.) Similarly, when a man is aroused by the sight of his wife getting undressed before bedtime, it would be helpful for her to learn to feel special in that she is desired by her husband. He's not a slobbering degenerate; he's a man created by God to be attracted to his wife's physical form. Now, men, that doesn't mean your wife wants to be pawed every time she changes clothes. But the private playfulness and physical flirting can not only be fun but can keep our intimacy interesting and adventuresome.

Tim: Women don't want quickies all the time, to be sure. But in a setting of love and respect, fast food can be a gift to their husbands. And gifts of love, like grace, are not demanded or expected; they are freely given.

Amy: Husbands should ask their wives, "What could I do for you to show you that you're special to me?" The answer probably won't be "Give me a steady diet of quick sex." It may be things like "Joyfully clean up the kitchen," "Be patient with the kids," or simply "Spend special time with me." It could even be a long, uninterrupted massage that doesn't end with intercourse. Those examples, however, may not mean anything to your wife. Some women would much rather receive a love note, a bouquet of flowers, or a night out, completely planned by their husband with a baby-sitter included. The important thing is to ask her and then act accordingly.

Tim: Now, in case you haven't already noticed, how much we talk isn't the only difference between the sexes. Women and men are also different in how they are stimulated, how they climax, and what they need in order to be sexually fulfilled.

Amy: Men are more compartmentalized. They can separate out their sexual thoughts and desires from the rest of their day. A husband can walk into a house full of screaming kids, a ringing phone, and a barking dog, and he'll still be thinking, *Tonight is going to be one exciting rendezvous.* Short of being comatose or in a full body cast, a man's sexual desire is largely unaffected by external factors.

Tim: A woman, on the other hand, is more holistic. If some part of the relationship is rocky, sex is usually not the first thing on her mind. If she and her husband had a disagreement that morning and they still haven't resolved the issue, that's a big barrier to her feeling sexy. She's also more easily distracted by her surroundings. A sick child, overnight guests sleeping just down the hall, teenagers up late watching a movie—factors like these need to be taken into account. That's why a woman wants the security of a locked door and a quiet setting.

Amy: Men are stimulated by sight, fragrance, touch, actions… Okay, men are just stimulated. Knowing this, ladies, go ahead and make use of the things that excite your mate. Wear sexy lingerie, dab on his favorite perfume, light candles, play music. Do whatever you both agree on to create a romantic atmosphere. It's not only okay to do so. It honors the celebration of this holy union we enjoy as husbands and wives.

Tim: Women are stimulated by tender words, loving actions, gentle touch. If a woman feels loved, cared for, protected, valued, listened to, supported, encouraged, not criticized, and almost worshiped—in a healthy sense—by her husband, she'll be more likely to give herself freely to him.

Our job is to learn and practice the habits that make our mates feel loved.[4] Our mission, given by God (especially to husbands in Ephesians 5:25), is to love our mates in a way that they experience love. And, as always, we don't do these things to receive love (or sex) in return. We do them because we are called to love our spouses.

DIFFERENCES GONE AWRY

Tim: It's important to look at some of the clinical aspects of the differences between male and female sex drives, and that list includes the differences in sexual arousal. I think a primary reason many men seem to be sexually stimulated all the time is because they have allowed their eyes to wander all day long. Thus, they get home in the evening with their motor already warmed up and ready to race to the finish line. Staring at lingerie ads, peering down low-cut blouses, and watching television shows that traffic in flesh keep men constantly on the edge of arousal.

I'm not saying it should be easy not to look; the problem is I don't see many men trying very hard not to. Colossians 3 tells us to "set your minds on things above" (verse 2) and to "put to death...whatever belongs to your earthly nature: sexual immorality, impurity, lust" (verse 5). These are disciplines that we husbands should practice. As we do that, as we allow our wives to be the exclusive source of our sexual stimulation (and we need to let her know that), we'll find that the male and female sex drives are not as far apart as we think.

Furthermore, many sources have said that sex is the primary way men feel loved, and that fact is reason enough for women to be more willing to engage in sex with passion. However, even if physical connection is the way a man feels most loved by his wife, that is not an excuse for nonstop sexual advances. Just like the many people who want to lose weight without watching what they eat or to be wealthy without hard work and financial discipline, many men want to feel loved by simply having sex without learning to share their hearts and serve their mates. Men may want women to grow in their willingness to engage sexually, but many men need to grow in their ability to express nonsexual love.

Now, I don't want to speed over that last point too quickly. Not the one about men needing to grow, but the one about many men wanting their wives to grow in their eagerness for sexual intimacy. If indeed physical intimacy is the way your husband feels most loved by you (or even a way), then it is important to examine your attitudes about sex before God. You must ask why you are not as eager or as interested as your mate. Part of that answer may lie in what we've been talking about: You have not felt loved by your husband in nonsexual ways and therefore do not feel fully valued for being more than a warm body in your sexual relationship.

However, another part of that answer may lie in your own fear of fully giving yourself to this experience, to fully trusting your mate (and God) in the arena of sacred sex. Let me ask you, if your husband felt most loved by you if you fixed him scrambled eggs, bacon, and biscuits for breakfast two days a week, would you do it? The fact that he could fix his own is irrelevant. The reality that some weeks you may only make the meal once due to external factors is irrelevant. The question is, If that's what makes him feel most loved, would you do it?

The reason I believe the breakfast is much easier than to be fully engaged sexually is the amount of personal cost. Whipping up breakfast isn't that big of a deal. I can do that, watch the news, and organize the kid's day all at the same time. But being sexually intimate *while being fully present in mind, body, and soul* is costly. It takes a huge part of you as a woman to do that. But you know what? It is that participation of the mind and soul—not the body—that makes your husband experience and feel your love and passion.

Yes, there is plenty of room for both husbands and wives to learn about love.

R-E-S-P-E-C-T

Amy: In the same passage in which Paul commanded husbands to love their wives, wives are commanded to respect their husbands (Ephesians 5:33). This respect must certainly show up in our sexual relationship. Wives, we need to admire our mates, encourage them, support them, believe in them, and let them know how highly we think of them. If we find that respect isn't there, we must ask ourselves why. And we must deal with the reasons.

Tim: Our wives certainly need respect as well. In a culture that too often ascribes value to women according to the firmness of their thighs or the size of their breasts, women need to feel that we don't just want their body, but that we want them as a person. Does this mean that a woman doesn't want to know that her husband is attracted to her body? Absolutely not. It's extremely important for a wife to know that it is *her* body alone that is pleasing to her mate. Solomon concludes a heartfelt statement of praise of his wife's physical appearance by saying, "All beautiful you are, my darling; there is no flaw in you" (Song of Songs 4:7). Solomon is so in love with her in every area of their lives that he praises her completely. As a result, she feels free from criticism, and she is truly able to give herself sexually.

REGULATING YOUR SEXUAL TEMPERATURES

Amy: I recently heard an interview with a man who had two wives. He said that it worked great because God designed the wives to meet each other's emotional needs and all he had to do was have sex with them. Besides wanting to see him sent to Antarctica, thousands of miles from the nearest woman, I felt sad for all three of them. They are truly missing out on what God meant sexual intimacy to be.

God made men and women different so that we could lovingly encourage and lead each other into new experiences and thereby know true spiritual oneness. We can't share our whole person if we leave out the verbal or the physical. That being the case, I'd like to ask wives a very important question: "What is your attitude toward sex?"

In 1 Corinthians 7, Paul wrote, "The wife's body does not belong to her alone but also to her husband" (verse 4)—and the reverse is true as well. He goes on to say, "Do not deprive each other except by mutual consent...so that you may devote yourselves to prayer" (verse 5). Paul's bottom line: "The husband should fulfill his marital duty to his wife, and likewise the wife to her husband" (verse 3). The word *duty* in this passage has been misunderstood and misused. In English, the word carries with it the idea of a dreaded obligation. That is far from the sense of the Greek term, which means "debt" or "payment of an obligation that is owed." God made us all with sexual needs. By meeting each other's needs, we are simply restoring something that is missing, we are providing something that our spouse needs.

This perspective is very convicting for me because Tim often jokingly accuses me of "overfunctioning." If I'm asked to take a dish somewhere, I'll take two or three. If I'm buying a gift, I'll drive to three or four places until I find just the right thing. Over the years I've learned that, although being conscientious and wholehearted is a good trait, I sometimes put so much energy and time toward a certain project that I don't have anything left for my family.

I'm still learning to take that trait and invest it in our marriage, even in our sex life. But I know that to experience sex in the way God intended women to, I must consider and approach physical intimacy as welcome celebration. Filling my husband's sexual needs is something I'm called to do. So I must ask myself, "How often have I 'overfunctioned' when planning a sexual encounter with Tim?" My honest answer: Not often enough. How about you? We do difficult things every day. Why should we shy away from applying ourselves to mastering the art of holy sex?

Tim: Now, men, let me ask you something: The last time you initiated sex and your wife declined, what was the emotional temperature between the two of you? Did you pout, roll away, grumble, say something critical or hurtful? Or did you reach out to her not for sex, but to show her that you care for her deeply *without* sex? Did you attempt to make her feel loved in the way that she needed right then?

Having mutually great sex will always make us feel closer to each other. The emotional temperature will go up. It's part of God's plan. But not having sex should not lower the temperature; all that does is punish. And that isn't part of God's plan. A holy act of love should never be twisted into a weapon used for punishment.

I can't count the wives who have come into my counseling office and expressed their frustration over sex with these words: "He's never satisfied!" This statement usually follows with her sharing about a time that she has either initiated sex or done something a little different (like enjoying a quickie before work). In the midst of the lovemaking, her husband made a comment like "Can we do this again tomorrow?" or worse, "Are you only initiating because I asked you to?" Come on, guys! As your wife reaches out to try to please you, you need to receive what she gives as a wonderful gift and be thankful. Don't be like a kid who now wants another cookie.

Remember, men, if orgasm is your goal, sex will always leave you wanting more—more frequency, more variety, more excitement. But if we men make oneness our goal, then we will be satisfied. Our wives will know it, and they will experience greater freedom to give themselves to us in lovemaking.

Now wives, I must ask you, if you have found answers to your questions about why God created sex, if you have prayerfully dealt with past and present issues that have been barriers to your giving yourself freely to your husband, and if your mate is truly trying to love you in a selfless way, then what is holding you back from giving yourself to this sacred experience? We have more to cover in this book that may help, but for some wives, the only issue now is fear; they are scared to trust God and take a step.

Remember Sarah from previous chapters? As we approached the end of therapy, having dealt with her issues of desire, her perceptions of sex, and her barriers, she finally said, "I guess the only thing left for me to do is just do it." She knew the time had come for her to step out and risk, trusting God by reaching our to her husband sexually. Do you need to, by faith, take that risk? God wants you to. Sarah is thrilled she did.

In the midst of all this, we must never forget that sex is meant to be fun. C. S. Lewis said, "If we ban laughter from the marriage bed, we let in a pagan goddess."[5] If we can't laugh with our mates—even at our sexual foibles—we'll miss so much of what God has for us. If sex has not become a performance or a platform for egos, then laughter comes easily.

Amy: Finally, I can't express strongly enough how important our own relationships with God are in this whole sexual experience. If my relationship with God is growing and I'm open to Him, communicating with Him, and growing in His grace, it's easy to want to serve my mate. If I've been ignoring God, though, it's all too easy for me to be selfish.

If you desire more insights into a woman's perspective of the sexual experience and how it is a gift only she can give, I encourage you to read *Intimate Issues,* by Linda Dillow and Lorraine Pintus.[6] It's a wonderful book on God's gift of sex to women and the roles that He calls them to.

Tim: And men, I mentioned earlier that one of the sexiest things you could ever do with your wife is pray with her. Keep your own spiritual life in order, but also take the lead in developing your spiritual intimacy with your wife. When we see our wives as complete beings, it's hard to pursue them for sex at the expense of everything else. As we pray together, we'll want true passion, not just sex.

Amy: Tim and I highly recommend that you and your spouse make what we call a Date to Communicate. Go to a place you both enjoy where you can be uninterrupted and talk about the issues we've discussed. Ask each other:

- What are some things I can do to make our sexual relationship more special?
- What are some things I need to stop doing that will make the experience better for you?

Your Date to Communicate about sex should happen several times a year. And remember, we're called to serve in the context of our mate's differences, not to try to change him or her.

Tim: After this discussion, we encourage you to write each other a love letter entitled *The Perfect Evening of Romance.* Describe in loving detail what that would be for you, including the twenty-four hours leading up to your time together. Describe all the things that would make you feel uniquely loved. Include your appreciation of the differences between you and your mate. But also remember that, in order for the recipient of the letter to feel loved, you must not try to force activities that might make him or her uncomfortable. We must teach our mates how to serve us, but we must do so while serving them. We must seek to know them and our differences. Not only must we accept those differences, we must completely accept our mate.

After you write and share your letters, answer them—and I don't mean in writing.

QUESTIONS FOR CONVERSATION

1. You both know that the two of you are different, but how much have you talked about those differences? In light of what you read in this chapter, discuss some of the more obvious differences between the two of you.

2. Discuss the common lies about sex that are mentioned in this chapter. Which of them have you fallen prey to? Do you believe that men naturally have a stronger sex drive than women? Share specific ways that you can learn to live above these lies and enjoy sex in light of God's truth.

3. Are you selfish? Yep, us, too. Without trying to justify your behavior, share with each other how selfishness has negatively affected your marriage, especially your sexual relationship. Create a plan for battling together the "me firsts"—and remember to give each other grace for occasional failures. Commit to work together and support each other in prayer.

4. God did create men and women to be different, but the differences discussed in this chapter are not meant to be absolutes. There are degrees of variation from couple to couple. Discuss gender differences that are particular to you and your mate.

What tension comes from these differences? What strengths do these differences give you as a couple?

5. Amy and I mentioned some actions and gestures that can communicate love, but these are our personal preferences. Tell each other, in specific terms, what communicates love and respect to you.

6. Discuss the two questions we listed at the close of this chapter. Verbally commit to accept and love your mate as he or she needs to be loved. Then write the letter—and, yes, answer it.

Chapter 7

True Sexual Freedom

Realizing That Boredom Is Not the Biggest Enemy of a Fulfilling Sex Life

> There is no norm in sex. Norm is the name of a guy
> who lives in Brooklyn.
>
> —DR. ALEX COMFORT

Freedom and fun just seem to go together. When I reflect on the adventures that have made the deepest impressions on me, each one offered an element of freedom: climbing a fourteen-thousand-foot peak in the Rocky Mountains, skydiving, snow and water skiing, even, many years ago, swinging on the king of all rope swings in my parents' backyard. All of these provided a liberating rush of adrenaline and the thrill of emancipation from the normal constraints of life. There was freedom, and it was fun.

I think I'm like most Americans in my great love of freedom and the high value I place on having fun. In fact, the pursuit of fun has become one of the greatest virtues of our culture. The motto for the Indiana state lottery is "Fun is good." The message: Risking your hard-earned cash on a game in which the odds are a million to one is a heck of a good time. (Really?) Fun is used to sell everything from gambling to hair implants to cars to beer. Even sex (or especially sex) is mostly touted in an atmosphere of fun.

And what about the freedom that fuels the fun? According to the hucksters, sexual freedom means no constraints and no boundaries beyond "my own desires." But that sort of fun comes at a great cost. One social commentator observed that as fun has become life's greatest goal, we've lost sight of such values as deepening relationships and developing long-term friendships.[1] When fun becomes the goal of sex, we pursue it at the expense of intimacy, passion, and long-term commitment. Sex that is pursued as a form of recreation will, after a while, even lose its sense of fun. When it's isolated from the rest of life, fun isn't good for a relationship; it's deadly. When we seek fun as the highest good, it robs sex of its joy.

JOYLESS SEX

How many times have you heard the standard advice that variety is the key to keeping vitality in your sex life? The argument goes something like this: "If you had the same thing to eat at every meal, you'd eventually tire of it. Likewise, you need variety in your sexual menu so that you and your partner won't get bored." Modern-day relationship guru John Gray has written that, "Without passion, sex becomes routine and boring. With the assistance of advanced bedroom skills and love, a couple can continue to experience great passion and fulfillment."[2]

The problem with Gray's advice is that it assumes that boredom is the biggest enemy to a fulfilling sex life, which, by extension, means that fun is the greatest good that comes from sex. His advice also suggests that new techniques designed to increase fun will also increase true passion. But that's a grave error. Sex is to be fun, for sure. But if we make fun the measuring stick by which we judge our sexual relationship, then we'll fall prey to the law of diminishing returns. And we'll never find true passion.

The law of diminishing returns states that if the sole focus of any activity is deriving pleasure and physical gratification (or fun), then the level of pleasure we gain from that activity will diminish with time. Therefore, to receive the same level of gratification that we enjoyed previously, we have to increase the pleasure stimuli. This principle explains why someone moves from one illegal narcotic to a stronger one; the old high no longer satisfies.

The law of diminishing returns applies to sex as well. When a couple starts dating with fun as the goal, simply holding hands produces a big thrill (at least it did in the old days). If they progress to kissing, they find that they no longer are satisfied with just holding hands. Then, if they move on to intimate caressing, kissing takes a backseat, and so forth. Once a couple engages in heavy petting, it's almost impossible for them to move back to just holding hands. The diminished thrill of holding hands no longer satisfies. That is, if fun is the goal.

The principle works the same way in marital sex. If pleasure and excitement are the standalone objectives of lovemaking, then having sex in the same way in the same setting will, at some point, become boring. Couples ordinarily seek to counteract that boredom by pursuing sexual variety, but after a while, that new pleasure diminishes as well. If one spouse isn't open to sexual variety, then his or her bored partner will seek greater frequency, trying to find satisfaction in quantity. Either way, a person is pursuing the same goal (sustaining the level of pleasure), but suffering the inevitable result (steadily diminishing returns). So, in the end, we either settle for being bored, or we seek new excitement and fun somewhere else. And if we seek more variety, eventually we will come up empty, just as the pursuit of more and more fun will prove to be a faulty path to a fulfilling sex life.

THREE LIES OF SEX

Our culture has sold us on three lies about sex. First, pleasure and fun are the highest goals of sex. Second, passion is sustained by variety. And third, sexual freedom means doing what I want when I want. These lies have created a culture with an insatiable sexual appetite—insatiable because of the law of diminishing returns. We're in the same situation that Paul described when he wrote about those who are separated from life in God: "Having lost all sensitivity, they have given themselves over to sensuality so as to indulge in every kind of impurity, *with a continual lust for more*" (Ephesians 4:19, emphasis added). How do these three lies about sex feed this "continual lust for more"?

Pleasure

If it's true that pleasure and fun are the highest goals of sex, then the purpose of sex is to achieve orgasm. According to this reasoning, since orgasm holds the promise of the greatest fun, orgasm alone gives sex meaning. This faulty logic is why many couples, when they're dating, blast right through things like cuddling and go straight to intercourse. But that, too, will eventually become boring. Each new level of sexual excitement will fail at some point, only to be replaced by something else that also will run its course and prove boring in the end. Making pleasure our goal will guarantee that we never reach that goal.

Passion

The lie that passion is created and sustained by sexual frequency and variety is far different from the truth experienced in sacred sex. Passion is actually conceived and enhanced through commitment, serving each other, and seeking the welfare of your spouse. Efforts to increase variety in a couple's sex life might temporarily stave off boredom, but it does nothing to create or deepen a couple's passion. True passion is built not on the continual pursuit of more variety, but on the enjoyment of all the little pleasures that sharpen the anticipation of being together.

Freedom

Sexual freedom has been wrongly understood as sex without limits and boundaries. It's falsely and selfishly defined as doing what I want when I want. Far from enhancing sexual pleasure, however, this approach only serves to make us lazy. This false notion of sexual freedom elevates personal needs and desires, serving to make sex a truly one-sided affair. Instead of leading us to explore with our spouse the sexual freedom we're given within marriage, this idea of freedom produces a self-centered sexual connection that is less about connecting than it is about gratifying one's own urges. True freedom is experienced when both partners enjoy sex within the boundaries of respecting one another's needs and preferences. In holy sex, we enjoy the freedom to serve our mates, not the license to exploit our mates.

Pleasure, variety, passion, and fun are not the goals of sex, but by-products of a mature, caring, God-honoring love life. The true goal of sex is a sacred, mysterious oneness. Fulfilling sex can only be an outgrowth of the genuine freedom that comes as another gift from a loving God.

THE HIGHEST LEVEL OF FREEDOM

The apostle Paul, a man whose life was characterized by a struggle between law and grace, wrote to the believers in Galatia, "It is for freedom that Christ has set us free. Stand firm, then, and do not let yourselves be burdened again by a yoke of slavery" (Galatians 5:1). Paul instructed believers that the grace of God through Christ has set them free from the enormous burden of trying to fulfill the requirements of the law. However, he warned them against letting their freedom lead them into sin: "You, my brothers, were called to be free. But do not use your freedom to indulge the sinful nature; rather, serve one another in love" (Galatians 5:13). We're reminded that we are free from the burden of the law, but that freedom is not a license to sin (see also Romans 6:1). Freedom brings with it responsibilities.

In his first letter to the Corinthians, Paul takes his argument a step further. After stating that believers are also exempt from following the laws concerning what they should eat and drink, he warned, "Be careful, however, that the exercise of your freedom does not become a stumbling block to the weak" (1 Corinthians 8:9). Christ has set me free from the burden of the law. My freedom, however, is not freedom to sin; even more, when it comes to things that God does *not* call sin, my behavior is governed by love for others. I am to put their well-being above my own desires. This is even more true in my marriage. I'm free to serve and love my mate in the ways that she most needs to be served and loved.

We've also been given freedom in our sex lives. As such, we are called, by the power of God's Spirit, to avoid sexual sin and to live within God's boundaries. We have complete sexual freedom within marriage, and it is governed by our love for the one to whom we are married. Freedom that is contained and governed by love is the highest level of freedom.

This sexual freedom is represented in several ways. One way is by our ability to be naked and unashamed with our spouse. In fact, being naked and unashamed means we can exercise sexual liberty with one another. We don't need to hide anything; we don't need to feel guilty or embarrassed; we don't need to feel self-conscious at all. But enjoying such freedom doesn't mean that all things are permitted. In writing about sex, theologian R. C. Sproul comments, "As [Russian novelist Fyodor] Dostoevsky said, 'If there is not a God, all things are permitted.' But [since] there is a God and his name is Yahweh and his Son is Jesus, then not all things are permitted, least of all selfishness."[3] The law of love therefore requires that when it comes to the fun aspect of sex, I need to be more concerned about my mate's fun than my own. Love limits our freedom and directs the way we approach fun in sex.

Holy sex is about loving, not using, and it is about unity much more than it is about fun. If sex is about fun first, it will lead us to demand more and more from our mates. We'll expect better performance, higher frequency, and more excitement. Ultimately, the pursuit of fun will have us demanding more of our mates than they are capable of giving. Or, as many women have decided, since the fun is not that great, they're willing to simply give up on sex. Their inner being tells them that abstinence is better than engaging in shallow, meaningless amusement.

If we pursue sex for the fun it brings, then we'll never experience the soul connection that is promised in this holy union. And without that depth of emotion, we cannot know true sexual freedom. The superficial pursuit of fun robs us of the genuine freedom God wants us to enjoy.

AVOIDING STATISTICAL MORALITY

Am I trying to argue that Christ-focused couples shouldn't experiment with sexual variety? Absolutely not! The freedom that God has given us to explore sexual pleasure—in our emotions, with our bodies, and in our spirits—is great indeed. But decisions regarding what occurs sexually between a wife and husband are theirs to make, free from the interference of outside cultural influences.

A couple should first determine what God allows and then what is right for them. To again quote R. C. Sproul: "Running through the popular sex manuals [to decide behavior] is the principle of what I call statistical morality. Ethical judgments are made on the basis of what is normal." But, as Sproul elaborates, choosing conduct based on what is "normal" for others in our society can lead to behavior that is an "expression of human corruption." Furthermore, God calls us to live "a life of nonconformity," even to "transform the statistical norm."[4] Therefore, the specifics of our sexual freedom can't start with statistics about what the average married couple does. Our sexual freedom must start instead with God and then be guided by His law of love.

It's not uncommon for Christ-focused couples to be told that within their own bedroom everything is permissible. As long as they engage in sexual practices only with each other, they can "throw off restraint and just go for it." Despite the great freedom that we enjoy, however, God gives us more guidelines than the one that prohibits adultery.

And the greatest guideline is to understand that sex is sacred. A reliable overall guide in this area of sexual freedom is indeed the "my mate only" principle. According to this principle, prolonged sexual stimulation produced by anything or anyone other than my mate violates the holiness of sexual intimacy. It's wrong because it damages the sanctity of oneness. I use the word *prolonged* because there will be occasions when we suddenly find ourselves sexually electrified in an unplanned encounter by something we see, hear, read, or remember. At the point of stimulation, however, we have a choice. We can turn those thoughts and emotions quickly toward our mates—thinking about the excitement generated by his or her words, form, and caresses—or we can allow our minds to dwell on the sexual stimulation aroused apart from our mates.

I know that advice based on the "my mate only" principle is incredibly tough for singles (believe me, I know—I didn't marry until I was twenty-eight) since there is not a mate to turn those thoughts toward. I know, too, that it's difficult even when we're married. Our minds fall for the deadly lie that sex with Person X will somehow be more fulfilling than it is with our mates. That myth is born out of a "sex for fun" mentality. But, married or single, if we are seeking sexual holiness, we can turn to God and ask for His strength. He doesn't leave us without an escape route from temptation (see 1 Corinthians 10:13).

The "my mate only" principle also answers a lot of questions that come up regarding sexual experimentation. *If we truly are free to enjoy sex without inhibitions,* some Christians wonder, *what about using stimulating magazines, adult videos, or erotic toys to heighten the experience?* I've even had clients ask, "What about thinking of something external that excites me while I'm having sex with my mate?" If you analyze that question, whenever something besides (or even in addition to) your spouse is giving you sexual stimulation while you're having intercourse, you are, in effect, using your spouse to masturbate. Then sex is not about two becoming one. It's about only one person: you.

You may be wondering about the ways to enhance the setting for sex discussed in chapter 6: candles, music, perfumes, and, of course, lingerie. Do these contradict the "my mate only" principle? No, they don't. Say, for example, that I come home from a tae kwon do workout wearing my sweat-drenched uniform. Instead of taking a shower, I simply put on a pair of dirty gym shorts and a ragged alumni T-shirt, eat a bag of lime tortilla chips with garlic salsa, and a few hours later crawl into our nice warm bed—without showering or brushing my teeth—and attempt to snuggle up to my wife? How attractive will my invitation be? That's okay. You don't have to answer. Really.

Showering, using cologne, and, yes, even wearing lingerie are simply gifts to our mates. Now I'm well aware of the complaint from wives whose husbands frequently buy them gifts that are actually gifts for the husband's personal enjoyment (I'm talking about lingerie here). We all know who will ultimately benefit from the "gift." There is a big difference between the wife who wears something to bed that she knows her husband will enjoy because it is her body in it and the wife who feels her husband only gets excited if she "dresses up" in order to enliven his adolescent fantasies. The principle, once again, is that your mate needs to provide the stimulation, not the mental associations connected with a lacy outfit. Husbands must find a way to clearly communicate to their wives, "It's you that I want to be with, just as you are, as God's gift to me."

So the margins of what is okay in marital sex must be evaluated by the principle of "my mate only." If a behavior or setting or mood enhancer violates that standard, then it can't be part of a pursuit of holy sex. Moreover—

and this is a prohibition in addition to adultery—any behavior that may cause physical or emotional harm is not okay, even if both partners agree to it. Anal sex is one example. As psychologist Everett Worthington Jr. states, "Sexual behaviors motivated by needs to debase the self aren't good.... Generally, whenever a person violates his or her values—whether consenting or not—there will be negative psychological effects."[5] Our freedom must always be placed in a setting of the human dignity and utmost consideration of our spouses, remembering that together we represent the image of the God of the universe.

ME, YOU, AND US

Nearly everyone has met someone who is considered the life of the party. These boisterous, outgoing individuals do and say things to make people laugh and have a good time. They seem to ooze self-confidence and appear to not care what others think of them. In reality, these party animals are often the most insecure people in the place. They believe they can only feel good about themselves when they can help others have fun. Far from being free from the constraints of what other people think, they instead feel that if people fail to have fun when they are around, then they are, in fact, a failure.

In order to be truly free to have fun in the encounter of holy sex, we must be free from judging ourselves according to what others think, including our mate's wants and desires. And we must be free to express our own wants and desires. The husband who asks, "Was it good for you?" is usually asking, "How good was I?" True freedom to have fun comes from having confidence in yourself and knowing and accepting how your mate is different from you.

In nearly all psychological theories, you'll find described a process (a battle, if you will) that we go through when we are in relationship with others. It's the tension we feel between our desire to be an independent individual and our conflicting desire to be in a close, intimate relationship with someone else. The struggle exists because if we move too far in either direction, we fear either an extreme independence that leads to isolation or being so enmeshed with another person that we lose all sense of self. The process to find a healthy balance is called differentiation.

Differentiation is the ability to be extremely close to someone else without losing a clear sense of your own identity. A differentiated individual is able to answer this question about emotions: "What's yours, what's mine, and what's ours?" I'm feeling this, you're feeling that, and together we feel this other thing. Differentiation is the ability to balance the desire for both intimacy and individuality. That may sound simple enough, but it's not.

Remember Michael and Sarah from chapter 2? Sarah is the wife whose sexual motto was one of resignation: "My husband needs sex, and it's my job to give it." Besides a failure to understand what are—and what are not—true male needs, Sarah and Michael had failed to differentiate themselves from each other in their sexual intimacy. Whenever Michael wanted sex (which seemed like all the time), Sarah confused his feelings with hers. She thought, "If he wants it, I must want it too." In truth, Michael's inability to differentiate produced the exact same thought in him: "If I want sex, she must want it too." Both had failed to realize that the mysterious oneness of holy sex must be entered into by personal choice, each one aware of his or her own feelings and sense of self. One mate's desire is not automatically a sign of the other mate's complementary feeling. We have separate needs, wants, and ideas about timing.

Michael and Sarah's task was simple to state yet profoundly difficult to live out. When Michael initiated sexual intimacy, Sarah had to learn that she had the freedom to meet him right where she was. If she was honestly too tired, she could say that. If she needed some time to find out what was going on in his world, she could say that. If she was distracted but chose to make love anyway, she needed to say that—all of that. And if she was as excited as he was at the prospect of connecting physically, she needed to share her enthusiasm, no holds barred. On the other side of the bed, Michael needed to hear Sarah's answers as coming from a wife who loved him and, no matter what, was not rejecting him as a man even if she didn't want to have sex just then. They both needed to know themselves.

If we are to maintain clear and separate identities, however, how can we truly be one in marriage? Being differentiated from our mates is not a contradiction to sexual intercourse making us "one." Sexual differentiation falls more under the category of sexual freedom. When it comes to the preferences, dislikes, and desires of our mates, we need to know and experience the freedom to be clear on what's yours, what's mine, and what's ours.

Remember Kevin and Brenda from chapter 3? They represent the huge strides in marital satisfaction that can be made when a wife and a husband shift their sexual focus from orgasm to oneness. After coming to believe that they desired not sex itself but a unique and spiritual connection with each other, they were ready to learn what it means to be sexually differentiated.

Kevin realized that Brenda loved being touched in certain ways during foreplay. Out of a desire to serve her, he chose to lovingly touch her in those ways even though it wasn't the most natural thing for him to do. Brenda knew that certain types of touching her were not Kevin's favorite form of foreplay, so she appreciated his efforts more than ever. She gladly received his touches as unconditional gifts.

Likewise, Brenda knew that Kevin got a tremendous enjoyment out of a particular sexual position. They both realized that, in that position, Brenda found it impossible to achieve an orgasm. However, she still enjoyed engaging sexually with Kevin in this position as a way of serving him. Neither one felt denigrated, neither felt used, neither felt an attitude of "Okay, I'll do this, but let's get it over with," and both felt loved and accepted.

As a sexually differentiated individual, you are able to communicate your likes, dislikes, and even things you are neutral on. And you are able to hear your mate's likes and dislikes without being offended or feeling judged. Someone who is differentiated is able to express a longing for sex without fearing rejection and without assuming that his or her mate wants the same thing within the same time frame. Conversely, if the spouse chooses not to want to engage for whatever reason, differentiation gives him or her the freedom to say no and not have it be interpreted as rejection.

This healthy scenario brings us back to the conventional wisdom regarding variety and experimentation in sex. Do we really need variety on the sexual menu? Having been granted the freedom to enjoy sex within God's law of love, couples are indeed free to explore new techniques and environments. However, if one of you desires a particular type of sex and your spouse just can't muster the willingness to give it a try, your mate doesn't have to do it! Now, it's probably hard for you to give up something you think would be fun because your mate is uncomfortable, but you must. If missing out on it bothers you that much, you've made fun a higher goal than oneness. But if you focus on oneness and holiness, you won't feel as if you are somehow being cheated out of the sexual fun that you think you deserve.

One more point. If you receive your sexual information primarily from the magazine rack at the grocery checkout lane, you'll believe things like "every man loves getting oral sex and every woman loves giving it." In reality, however, studies show that this is not true.[6] A majority of women do not like giving or receiving oral sex, and most men don't find it the most enjoyable way to engage sexually. The reason everybody is talking about it is simply because everybody is talking about it.

Kevin, for instance, certainly needed to consider the source of his ideas and desires for sex. He'd watched too many adolescent-focused movies that made oral sex seem like something that every man needed to have and something every woman wanted to give. The exaggerated stories of the sexual exploits of an unmarried coworker added fuel to the fire. Brenda had no real moral reason for not wanting to engage this way, and there was not an abusive event from her past that colored her thinking. She simply didn't like it. Oral sex caused her to lose all sexual arousal. As she became differentiated, though, she learned that she had the freedom to say no, and Kevin learned that other sexual encounters are far more fulfilling.

Combined with the law of love, self-differentiation allows you to know and serve your mate in a way that seeks only the best for him or her. It also gives you the ability to feel comfortable with your own preferences, rather than feeling judged for desiring something different. Ultimately, however, differentiation will keep you from feeling as if you're missing out if your spouse doesn't want to do something. Your sense of who you are, apart from your mate, is actually strengthened when you serve your mate by denying your own desires.

THE FREEDOM TO SAY NO

Here's another adage that applies to holy sex: You can't truly say yes to sex until you can say no. I've had many clients who feel that it's wrong to say no to their mate when it comes to sex. They've all found *nonverbal* ways to say no—going to bed early or late, feigning sleep or sickness, men having to work, or women deciding that they must be beginning their period. I've also found that most of these people can't say yes to sex either. They don't tap into the power of a glad willingness to engage with their partner. They may acquiesce, but they don't say yes with enthusiasm.

If we can feel free to say no, where does that leave the idea of submission in marriage? First, submission never means doing what you're told. In relationships between believers, between spouses, and even in sex, the principle is always "Submit to one another out of reverence for Christ" (Ephesians 5:21). In short, submission means to willingly put another's interests ahead of our own. In holy sex, God has given us great freedom, but the principle of submission doesn't allow either partner to demand anything sexually from their mate, either in frequency or in type of sexual activity. As Gary Smalley writes, "At the heart of love is a decision to honor a person—to count him or her as incredibly valuable. Forcing my wife to violate her conscience to please my sexual appetite is absolutely wrong and an invitation to sexual problems."[7] Submission can't be construed to mean that either spouse is required to violate his or her conscience when it comes to sexual expression.

In the holiness of sex, we give our minds, our bodies, and our hearts—our whole selves—to our mates as a gift. To be a gift, we must be able to say, "Yes, I want to do this. I want to be one with you." If sex is regarded as an obligation, we'll never enter into it freely the way God intended. Very often, the hesitancy to say yes is due to a variety of past experiences and to current thoughts that make someone feel that if they say yes, they are agreeing to do something that is wrong or agreeing to being hurt—and neither one is what God desires.

People who have suffered the trauma of sexual abuse may feel if they verbally say yes to sexual intimacy, they are saying yes to being abused again. By not verbalizing, they remove themselves from responsibility in the current encounter because to say yes to being abused again is unconscionable. Through therapy and by God's grace, they can learn to say yes to intimacy with their mate and know that it's not abuse, but God's gift as they separate the past from the present. Other individuals may, because of previous experiences, feel that sex is simply a way they were used (or used others) in the past and therefore saying yes now is repeating those old patterns. When people feel that their body and all its sexual components are there to be used at another's demand, they normally have difficulty saying yes because they never felt that their no was respected. In sacred sex, it will be.

So on your journey into the holiness of sex, pray for God's healing that you can say a joyous, wholehearted yes to your mate. And then know it's also okay to say no, knowing your mate will continue to love you, uninterrupted, and without pouting.

THREE SEXUAL ENCOUNTERS

I like to think of healthy marital sexual encounters in three categories, and I liken those categories to dining at three different restaurants. (Okay, it may sound weird, but if you've read this far, that shouldn't surprise you.) The first grouping is Fast-Food Sex. This primarily includes "quickies" and those spur-of-the-moment rendezvous that take place without a lot of planning. Frequently, only the husband will have an orgasm (though not always). Fast food is fine, on occasion, but too much of it will leave one or both of you lacking passion and feeling taken for granted just as too many triple cheeseburgers will leave you—well, let's just say, not healthy.

The second category is Informal Dining. Here, you take the time to decide where you want to go, order what you want from the menu, and enjoy a lengthy time of uninterrupted togetherness. In holy sex, this should be the most frequent experience. This is not necessarily planned sex, but as some of you know, sexual spontaneity and parenthood are often diametrically opposed. For you parents to have a time of intimacy with an unrushed schedule and an unencumbered mind is rarely something that "just happens." This kind of encounter almost always requires some planning.

Informal Dining sex means you both are participating, both feeling waited on, and both experiencing what you enjoy, even if your enjoyment is from what your mate is experiencing. It's common for both partners to experience orgasm though, as always, orgasm is not the goal; oneness is. At this restaurant, your mate matters to you, and you know that what matters to you matters to your mate. You come away from the experience feeling connected, feeling loved, and feeling satisfied.

The final category is Five-Star Dining. This is coat-and-tie, linen-tablecloth, reservations-required dining. For the majority of folks, this is not a weekly or even a monthly event. However, as we grow in our understanding and ability to live out all aspects of God's gift of sexuality, we will dine here sexually more often than we can afford to dine there for food.

More than planning, fine dining takes commitment. Just as eating at a fifty-dollar-per-plate restaurant takes a pledge of saving for the special occasion, experiencing passion on this level takes three vital commitments. First, this type of intimacy can be achieved only when you know that your mate is committed to you unconditionally and accepts you completely. Only in this type of mutual commitment can the two of you experience true sexual freedom.

The second commitment is simply to make Five-Star Dining happen. A sexual connection at this level is the culmination of hours, even days (including a married lifetime), of cherishing and being cherished. It can occur on a lazy weekend that began by sleeping in together, sharing a cup of coffee, working together on a project, or watching an old movie while snuggling in front of the fireplace. It's more likely to happen on a night that has taken considerable preparation and, more important, created the anticipation. Those who saved the consummation of their marriage until their wedding night know what it is to share feelings of excited anticipation.

A night like this may involve attending a wedding and a reception where there is dancing and celebration, a weekend overnight getaway, or a party with friends. It will be a time when secret (emphasis on secret) signals were sent, when there was flirting, looks, touches, kind words. Five-Star Dining could begin with playing a game that is geared toward getting to know your spouse better (some of these games are morally sound; others are trash). It could involve a book that gives creative romance hints or a Christian resource like *Simply Romantic Nights*, available through Family Life Today.[8] It might entail a shared bubble bath, a long period of simply being close, or a moonlit stroll.

A Five-Star Dining encounter doesn't mean that intercourse lasts all night. Sexual intercourse may actually take less time than a quickie, but the expectation and the intensity are different. You both arrived at your time of celebrating oneness feeling aroused, knowing you were connected, confident that this person whom you love with all your being loves you the same way. This longing for each other can never happen by simply falling into bed and having sex. This creative expectancy is the only setting in which the term *making love* accurately applies.

If we prayerfully seek to uphold the "my mate only" principle, bolstering it by pursuing and maintaining the holiness of sexual intimacy, then we can bring peaceful togetherness to the potential battlefield of what to do in the bedroom. As we become healthily differentiated, we will find freedom to both serve and to be incredibly close to our mate. All along, our guiding questions must be the following: Does this behavior promote oneness? Am I loving and valuing my mate? Am I making passion a commitment and a priority? Am I seeking unity first, and have I put freedom and fun in their proper place?"

It's not that fun is bad. But it's our freedom to love each other sacrificially, our freedom to serve and lovingly be one, that God declares "very good." And guess what? It will lead to some of the greatest fun you've ever had.

QUESTIONS FOR CONVERSATION

1. Unless you've lived on another planet for the past decade, you have encountered the three lies of sex discussed at the beginning of this chapter. Which of them have affected you and your spouse? Honestly share together how these lies have impacted your sexual relationship.

2. Talk about pleasure, passion, and freedom. Make sure each of you shares one thing about each area that you believe would increase your intimacy in a way that is honoring to God and to your mate.

3. Has your relationship suffered from statistical morality? If so, explain how. In what ways have you embraced and experienced the freedom that God has given you within the boundaries of your marriage? How and why have you failed to experience that freedom? Together develop a plan to increase the experience of godly freedom and fun in your sexual intimacy.

4. Do you feel the freedom to say no and yes when it comes to sex? Talk about recent occurrences of each. Also share what has been difficult for you when it comes to saying yes or no to intimacy. What can your spouse do to help you overcome this obstacle?

5. Find a place where no one can hear you and discuss the three restaurants of sexual fun and freedom. Where do you dine most often? Where would you like to dine more? Have you ever experienced the sexual equivalent of Five-Star Dining? If so, share your memories of this time. If you haven't, when are you going to make a reservation? What commitments will you make in order to keep that reservation?

Chapter 8

The Truth About Our Bodies

Finding the Bible's Definition of "Supermodel"

> The fact that we have bodies is the oldest joke
> there is.
>
> —C. S. LEWIS

In the hit movie *City Slickers,* three friends from New York City sign up for a cattle drive in an attempt to cheat their fleeting youth. They think the macho adventure will prove they haven't lost any of their virility.

In one scene, Mitch (Billy Crystal) and his buddies discuss a moral dilemma. Mitch's friend has just implied that it's every man's prerogative to look at a beautiful woman. As they debate the point, it comes down to this question: If the most beautiful woman you ever saw got out of a spaceship and all she wanted to do was have the greatest sex in the world with you and then she would get back on the ship and fly away so no one would ever know, would you do it? After a few one-liners, Mitch makes his pronouncement: "It wouldn't make it right if [my wife] didn't know; I'd know, and I wouldn't like myself."

At first, this seems like a morally upright answer. A man should do what he knows inside is the right thing. But psychologist Gary Brooks, author of *The Centerfold Syndrome,* points out that the whole situation ignores an even greater question: "Why would a man want to have intimate sexual relations with someone he didn't know anything about, had nothing in common with, and would never see again? Why would any man in his right mind even consider it?"[1]

The answer that our culture supplies is the same rationale Mitch's friend used: Because she's the most beautiful woman you've ever seen.

BEAUTY WORSHIP

If there's anything in our society besides sex that has reached critical overload, it's a topic that is almost always associated with sex: our bodies. It's no exaggeration to say that everywhere we are bombarded with messages about how bad our bodies are and how good they could be if we just purchased the right products or paid for the right procedures. In today's mail I read a health club ad claiming that "some people don't realize that the potential for a great body is just around the corner." Of course, the women pictured in the ad were thin and large-breasted, and all of them were wearing the latest revealing leotards. When you consider all the advertisements, infomercials, magazines, and movies, you realize we're the targets of a staggering daily assault of body worship.

And yet, within this barrage of beautiful bodies all promising sexual fulfillment, we don't hear what I believe to be the most accurate description of our bodies. Saint Francis of Assisi taught a healthy way to regard our own bodies, and we need to adopt his view if we are to freely use our bodies in the gift of holy sex. Saint Francis referred to his body simply as "Brother Donkey"—useful but certainly not worthy of worship.[2]

In commenting on Saint Francis, C. S. Lewis points out that "no one in his right senses can either revere or hate a donkey."[3] No one prizes it for its beauty, nor denies its usefulness. It can be frustrating, funny, lovable, and, at times, worthy of praise. It is not, however, paraded in beauty contests, lusted after on the Internet, or subjected to the artificial enhancements of cosmetic surgery. It is, my friends, a donkey.

Sensible, right? And yet this perfectly reasonable view of the human body is unheard of today. Instead, we have a society that is consumed by the quest to possess the perfect body. According to the American Board of Plastic Surgery, board-certified plastic surgeons performed 1.5 million procedures in 1998, up 153 percent from 1992. The four most common procedures, in order, are liposuction, breast augmentation, eyelid surgery, and face-lifts.[4] This statistic does not include the figures for many states where physicians who are not board certified perform various cosmetic procedures. Furthermore, since many procedures take place in the office and are paid for out of pocket, the actual amount spent on plastic surgery is difficult to determine. We can rest assured, however, that it's in the multi-billions.[5]

For those who avoid the extremes of the knife, there is the $33-billion-dollar weight-loss industry.[6] According to the federal government, 25 percent of American men and almost 40 percent of American women are trying to lose weight,[7] and some sources say more than 50 percent of women are on some type of diet.[8] Whether the advertisements are for pills or the latest fad diet, millions of dollars are spent each year to get us to use a product that promises to change our bodies. Of course, this advertising statistic doesn't even touch on those who go the route of exercise, where another $5 billion a year is spent on home workout equipment, a 163-percent hike from 1990, and $8 billion more (some estimates are double that) spent on health club memberships.[9] And none of these figures include the $70 billion spent annually on cosmetics.[10]

Although the majority of marketing for the Industry of Appearance targets women, men have found their own place in the limelight. Though a muscular physique and a six-pack stomach are greatly cherished, the higher prize seems to have become a full, flowing head of hair. With egos to be stroked and money to be gained, hair replacement has become an annual $1 billion industry.[11] With assurances of renewed confidence and implied promises of bikini-clad babes on your arm, why should you put up with embarrassing hair loss?

THE BUSINESS OF BEAUTY

Much of the $187 billion that is spent each year on advertising in the United States.[12] is specifically intended to convince us that, if we looked different, we'd not only be happier people, but we'd be better people. Slogans for cosmetic surgery clinics suggest that an improved physical appearance really does make someone an improved person. Less subtle is the message that looking better is the fast track to fulfilling sex. In other words, if you were just a little better looking and lost a little weight, you'd have a heck of a lot better sex life.

Combine the quest for physical beauty with the fact that North American retail sales of romance novels have grown from $700 million in 1995 to more than $1 billion a year in 2000.[13] Next throw in the manner in which romance and sex are portrayed throughout the entertainment industry. Then take a look at the magazine covers bombarding us with sexual misinformation every time we buy groceries. What do we have? A big, misleading, damaging sexual mess.

Here's what we learn from our cultural circus: For women, sexy is thin—very thin—with large (or at least firm) breasts and the willingness to reveal absolutely as much skin as allowed by law. Sagging breasts, large hips, and any fat cells are taboo. Sexy means you're free from blemishes, wrinkles, and stretch marks. For men, sexy is a full head of flirtatiously styled hair, well-defined muscles, and, of course, no shirt. For both men and women, it's tanned skin, a toned, firm body, and perfect, brightly whitened teeth. And, as important as anything, sexy is young. In a word, sexy is perfect.

But the lie doesn't stop there. Get ready for part two: People with flawless bodies have incredible sex. I'm talking about screaming, mountaintop passion anytime they feel like it, anyplace they want. These perfect people are having the sex you long for, but because you're not perfect, you'll never get it unless you get out your credit card and buy the product.

We should see through this transparent ploy to empty our bank accounts, but we just keep swallowing it. We actually believe as a culture, even if we'd never admit it, that sex is better for people who possess what our culture defines as the perfect body.

A BETTER BEAUTY

I'm not out to abolish all diets, exercise, cosmetics, and surgeries. But for those who participate (myself included) in any of the aforementioned activities, we must answer one question in light of God's gift of our mates and the holy celebration of sex: Why are we doing it?

If you've suffered any type of physical disfigurement, either by birth, injury, or illness, or if there's some other type of corrective cosmetic surgery you and your doctor think is advisable, then you have valid reasons to pursue surgery. If your doctor tells you to lose twenty pounds and watch your diet because of blood pressure, then the "why" answers are clear: You'll be healthier and you'll live longer. If you join a health club to increase cardiovascular health, to get in shape for the church basketball league, or to combat job stress, you've made a good choice. If you feel more comfortable getting a new hairstyle or wearing makeup, then by all means, do it.

However, if the subtle motivation is that somehow you'll have more worth as a person, then you're wasting your time and your money. If you're convinced that you'll be more lovable, a better person, or more valuable to others if your appearance is altered, you will ultimately be disappointed. If you believe that having bigger breasts, a tighter stomach, or a fuller head of hair will increase your sexual enjoyment and that your emotional intimacy will skyrocket, you've bought into the "great bodies equal great sex" lie. It's time to hear the truth.

ESCAPE THE CULTURAL QUAGMIRE

God's truth in this regard has been vindicated by modern experience. One of the most prophetic voices speaking God's truths into our culture is Richard Foster. In discussing God's call to believers to pursue a life of simplicity in a possession-rich culture, Foster writes:

> Because we lack a divine Center our need for security has led us into an insane attachment to things. We really must understand that the lust for affluence in contemporary society is psychotic. It is psychotic because it has completely lost touch with reality. We crave things we neither need nor enjoy. "We buy things we do not want to impress people we do not like." Where planned obsolescence leaves off, psychological obsolescence takes over. We are made to feel ashamed to wear clothes or drive cars until they are worn out. The mass media have convinced us that to be out of step with fashion is to be out of step with reality. It is time we awaken to the fact that *conformity to a sick society is to be sick.*[14] (emphasis added)

Foster's point applies equally to our cultural obsession with the appearance of our bodies, the donkey referred to by Saint Francis. The belief that physical beauty guarantees happiness has reached a mindless and unethical extreme. The *New York Times* reported a plan to auction off the ova of supermodels, regardless of any other characteristic of the egg donor, so that couples could try to produce a beautiful child. It was later speculated that the Web site sponsoring the auction was actually a scam designed to bilk membership money and lure people onto a pornographic Web site. However, even though everybody from the American Society for Reproductive Medicine to the *New York Times* itself blasted the proposal, the concept of buying the eggs of "beautiful people" is not illegal. Sadly, the site recorded millions of hits; even more sad, people placed bids. The practice of engineering babies for physical beauty is a form of mass psychosis, and it's past time we awaken to the fact that conformity to a sick society is indeed to be sick.

Throughout the New Testament, believers are called to live above what is going on in the surrounding culture. We are to be in the world but not of the world (John 15:19). We are not to "conform any longer to the pattern of this world, but be transformed" (Romans 12:2). We are to realize that "beauty is fleeting" (Proverbs 31:30) and that "beauty should not come from outward adornment" (1 Peter 3:3). We need to live out "the unfading beauty of a gentle and quiet spirit" (1 Peter 3:4), which is God's standard. Then we'll find peace, security, and wholeness. And in that context we'll begin to discover the experience of holy sex that the world is so desperately seeking.

A CULTURAL REALITY CHECK

Beauty is not an absolute concept. The looks we worship today will be vilified in a few years as they give way to yet another "new look." Visit a museum that displays paintings by Gothic, Renaissance, and Baroque period artists. You'll find an obsession with bodies and especially the female form. As you look at paintings and sculptures from the fifteenth through the eighteenth centuries, you see exceptionally beautiful women. However, by today's standards, they all—including Venus, the very definition of an exceptionally beautiful woman—would be considered overweight by as much as thirty pounds. All of these models of female beauty have large hips, and most have small, "compact breasts."[15] The celebrated image of beauty for hundreds of years fit the widely ridiculed "pear shape" that today's woman is made to feel ashamed of.

Some people may argue that heavier, small-breasted women were considered beautiful because, in past centuries, that meant they were wealthy, had plenty to eat, and had servants to nurse their children. To that, I would say, "Exactly!" These paintings depict physical beauty according to a *subjective cultural definition.* The women who were considered sexually attractive then are the same women that our culture regards as not sexy today because their breasts aren't perfect and they look as if they've eaten a well-balanced meal.

The same kind of change in the standards of beauty has repeated itself much more recently. Look at the movie stars that have made pin-up status over the last seventy-five years. From the 1920s flapper with bound breasts to the voluptuous 1950s sex goddess Marilyn Monroe to the waiflike, "heroin chic" Kate Moss of more recent vintage, our definition of female beauty has been capricious and has flown in the face of God's creative prerogative. As a matter of fact, Marilyn Monroe, the woman who was beauty personified in the minds of many, would be considered overweight by today's standards.[16]

Not only does current thinking on beauty look down on large hips, but there's an absolute obsession with breasts. This lusting after the perfect breast is also a culturally created phenomenon. Marilyn Yalom, a senior scholar at Stanford University, writes:

> For most of us, and especially men, the breasts are sexual
> ornaments—the crown jewel of femininity. Yet this sexual-
> ized view of the breast is by no means universal. In a num-
> ber of different cultures in Africa and the South Pacific,

where women have gone about with their breasts uncovered since time immemorial, the breast has not taken on the predominately erotic meaning it has in the West. Non-Western cultures have their own fetishes—small feet in China, the nape of the neck in Japan, the buttocks in Africa and the Caribbean.[17]

Socialization within a culture defines the most desirable physical shape and size, and even the female body part that sexually excites an individual. As believers we can, by God's grace, live above our culture. Our lust over perfect bodies has been conditioned, and God can recondition us. Take comfort in the fact that the models who expose their breasts and stomachs today in print or on screen would not even have made the first cut as candidates to model for the great artists of the Gothic, Renaissance, and Baroque eras. Their lack of softness and their unnatural proportions would have been considered about as appealing as, well, a donkey.

BEAUTY AND GOOD SEX?

After we come to grips with our culturally influenced lust for physical perfection, we need to recognize the absurdity of linking beautiful bodies and sexual pleasure. Do we *really* believe that orgasm is more fulfilling when having sex with a large-breasted woman or that sex will be much more satisfying with a man who isn't bald? The idea would be funny if it weren't so tragic.

In light of these wrong-headed scenarios, we realize that a great many people have actually conditioned themselves to become sexually aroused. We accept as a given that men are stimulated by the sight of women's breasts, but this cause-and-effect relationship is culturally determined and is enhanced by a lack of discipline on the part of most men. As psychologist Gary Brooks writes: "This mania, this explosion in glorification and objectification of women's bodies, promotes unreal images of women, distorts physical reality, creates an obsession with visual stimulation, and trivializes all other natural features of a healthy psychosexual relationship."[18]

Those "other natural features" of healthy sex gain strength as our thoughts turn to our mates as being beautiful just as they are and as being God's gift to us. When we enter into the mysteries of marriage with our mates and as we get to know them on the inside, the very thought of them will bring pleasure sexually, and that's the only type of sexual stimulation and encounter that will last beyond orgasm. We'll come to realize that the fantasy of having anonymous sex with a gorgeous space alien would be a meaningless, unfulfilling experience. But making love to our mates can be an incredibly fulfilling endeavor for an entire lifetime.

DIMINISHING RETURNS

In the previous chapters, I discussed the law of diminishing returns. In sex, this law means that if we focus on orgasm as the goal of sexual activity, then the level of pleasure will diminish with time. Each new position or stimulation aid will only provide added excitement for a while. Then it, too, will fail to satisfy fully. This same law also applies to the cultural concept of the human body's role in sex.

Kevin and Brenda, who were struggling with several areas of marital dissatisfaction in chapters 3 and 7, enjoyed a jump-start to their sexual passion when they began to view it as an experience of holy worship and as they allowed God to become the foundation of their marriage. Eighteen months later, however, they were back in my office. Their passion was once again in decline. Within four months after we'd stopped meeting together, they had allowed their schedules to consume them. Their personal interactions had dwindled to calendar synchronization, and their times of sharing their hearts were almost nil. Despite Brenda's requests for nonsexual hugs, Kevin had returned to grabbing her and groping like a schoolboy. During their imes of sexual intimacy, he was again focusing on orgasm instead of oneness.

Kevin knew something was wrong. But instead of working to build spiritual intimacy with Brenda (he said they were doing better spiritually than Brenda reported), he thought they needed something "new" to spice up their love life. With the locker-room mentality of a fourteen-year-old, Kevin concluded that Brenda's breasts were too small. Surrounded by lots of Kevins all her life, Brenda had always been self-conscious about being less endowed than many women. With the passion gone and Kevin convinced that small breasts were a turnoff, Brenda agreed to a breast augmentation.

To be honest, Brenda's new look, combined with the created need for some new lingerie, did produce increased passion. For a while, Brenda felt sexier. For a while, Kevin was more attentive to his wife outside the bedroom. For a while, they both experienced a higher level of sexual satisfaction. They both experienced the sexual passion they were looking for—for a while. Then the law of diminishing returns performed its work, and they were back in my office.

BELIEVERS IN THE SNARE

Sadly, there are many couples like Brenda and Kevin. And sadder still, many of the church's teachers have unwittingly supported our culture's beauty worship. I've heard prominent Bible teachers tell women, "If the house needs painting, paint it" in reference to the need to wear makeup. I've read books in which Christian authors advise cosmetic surgery even for a "beauty only" purpose. Once again I remind you: To be conformed to a sick society is to be sick.

It's amazing how much the church has bought into our culture's obsession with looks. It's time for us to grow up and accept one another as people, not as physical specimens. A man needs to be able to proclaim about his bride, "How beautiful you are, my darling! Oh, how beautiful!" (Song of Songs 1:15). And this joyous exclamation is very different from stating that his wife measures up to some subjective cultural standard.

I once heard a pastor in Texas tell about a couple who had come to see him for counsel. They were deep in financial debt but were considering a major purchase that would put them another five thousand dollars in the red. The item to be bought? A fur coat. The justification for "needing" one? To not feel out of place—on Sunday morning in church. Remember, this is in south-central Texas where a fur coat could only be worn six to eight times a year at most. In challenging the process of justification that we believers go through to fit into our culture, the pastor concluded his sermon by saying, "If one more person comes up to me and says, 'We're putting in a pool so we can have the church youth group over to swim,' I'm going to come over to your house and throw up in your pool. If you want a pool, put it in, but don't try and justify it to me. Justify it to God."

Financially successful men justify leaving their mate of twenty years because they feel they deserve a "trophy wife." Women justify starving themselves because they fear being too fat. Men justify having an affair because their wife's body no longer excites them. Women justify cosmetic surgery because it makes them feel sexier and they fear not looking youthful. Don't justify it to the culture; justify it to the God who said that what He brings together in marriage, no one should separate (Mark 10:9).

Just like our *City Slickers* cowboy friends trying to recapture their fleeting youth, the problem for women seeking that same path is simple: It's impossible to stay young. If a woman has a child, her hips will expand, her breasts will lose their firmness, her stomach will have stretched (most likely leaving marks), and she will have endured approximately twenty-five times more pain than her husband can even imagine. Furthermore, the average woman in America is five feet four inches tall and weighs 142 pounds, while the top models are five feet nine inches tall and weigh between 110 and 118 pounds.[19] These statistics show that only 5 percent of all American women actually meet the "ideal." We live in a sick culture, and we need God to make us well.

In *The Centerfold Syndrome,* Gary Brooks writes, "As the culture has granted men the right and privilege of looking at women, women have been expected to accept the role as stimulators of men's visual interest, with their bodies becoming objects that can be lined up, compared, and rated."[20] To judge a woman solely by her looks is nothing short of sinful. It stands in complete opposition to the biblical standard of a woman's beauty: "Your beauty should not come from outward adornment, such as braided hair and the wearing of gold jewelry and fine clothes. Instead, it should be that of your inner self, the unfading beauty of a gentle and quiet spirit, which is of great worth in God's sight" (1 Peter 3:3-4). The true worth of every woman is that she is a creation of the Most High God, and the beauty of her spirit, not her ability to reach an unattainable cultural standard, is what God sees as true worth.

CRAWLING OUT OF THE SWAMP

Our culture's obsession with thinness has not only caused trouble in marriages and an objectification of women, but it has also ushered in an explosive increase in the number of eating disorders, an ailment that affects women at a rate nine times higher than it affects men. Stories such as that of Courtney Thorne-Smith, the thirty-three-year-old actress who left the television series *Ally McBeal* after losing too much weight and realizing she was harming her health, are all too common. Thorne-Smith says she felt pressured by the media, by the entertainment profession, and even by male actors who told her how "good" she looked when she was starving herself. She later thanked God that "my life is more important to me than my weight."[21] She has regained between ten and fifteen pounds and feels good about herself, although she admits that body image issues still weigh on her mind.

Because of the emptiness and diminishing returns that result in our sex lives when we focus too intently on the culture's definition of beauty, more couples than I could estimate have been robbed of the true pleasures and joys of holy sexuality. If we are to experience not only godly sexuality but also "the peace of God, which transcends all understanding" (Philippians 4:7) in all aspects of our lives, we must live—and let others live—free from the cultural definition of beauty. In the words of Paul, we must "not conform any longer to the pattern of this world, but be transformed by the renewing of [our] mind. Then [we] will be able to test and approve what God's will is—his good, pleasing and perfect will" (Romans 12:2). And I'm convinced that His will is that we see our husbands and our wives with eyes that grant all people the worth that comes from God.

Society praises the beautiful body, but God sees physical beauty as fleeting and praises those who fear Him (Proverbs 31:30). Society looks at outer adornment, but God looks at the "inner self" (1 Peter 3:4). Society worships a beautiful woman regardless of any other qualities she may or may not have, but God sees a beautiful woman who lacks wisdom and discretion as a pig with a gold ring in her nose (Proverbs 11:22). Society sees beauty as a youthful, perfectly sculpted physique, something that is worth paying any price to achieve, but God knows that beauty among true lovers is borne out of passion, commitment, admiration, character, and a choice to see your lover as God's gift who fulfills every true need you have. By understanding God's perspective on beauty, we can say with Solomon:

> All beautiful you are, my darling;
> there is no flaw in you. (Song of Songs 4:7)

The price of that beauty is worth more than rubies (see Proverbs 31:10). Our bodies are a gift from God, designed by Him to be "living sacrifices, holy and pleasing to God" (Romans 12:1). Furthermore, as wives and husbands seeking to honor the One who created love, marriage, and sex, we are to let our bodies be gifts to our mates in a holy celebration (1 Corinthians 7:3-5). Our bodies are wonderful just as they are because, as believers, God sends His Holy Spirit to live in them; therefore our bodies are temples of God (1 Corinthians 6:19). (By the way, this passage explains that we should avoid sexual sin because our bodies are too holy to involve them in something so dishonoring to God.) And our bodies are wonderful because they are created in God's image.

OUR BODIES AND HOLY SEX

Someone much wiser than I am once said, "If a woman is beautiful before the age of forty, she had something to do with it. If she is beautiful after the age of forty, her husband had something to do with it." Now before I get pelted for speaking out of both sides of my mouth, realize that the beauty referred to in this proverb is a beauty of overall countenance. It describes a woman who exudes peacefulness, contentment, and confidence.

During the first forty years of a godly woman's life, her focus on building the life her heavenly Father has called her to makes her beautiful. After the age of forty, as she moves toward middle age, much of her countenance is determined by the love, support, and acceptance of her husband. If she has aged gracefully because, in part, of the blessed gift of unconditional love and acceptance from a husband who truly cherishes her, she will be beautiful. If she feels nagged, judged, and rejected, she won't. This is not a sexist statement; it's simply the truth. This certainly applies to single women as well. A single woman who has built her worth on the fact that she is a beautiful creation of God and continues throughout her life to surround herself with a body of believers who love and accept her for who she is will, indeed, be beautiful.

And the same is true for men. Although women suffer the brunt of our culture's body idolatry, men are by no means unaffected. The wife who is constantly on her husband about his weight, his physique, or his hairline—be it through confrontation or sarcasm—will grow in him ample insecurity. He, too, will be robbed of the gifts of freely encountering the love of an accepting wife and joyously experiencing the God-given blessing of holy sexuality.

Again, I'm not making a case against taking care of ourselves. Our bodies are the temples of God, and we should treat them as such. We should want to present our bodies at their best to our mate and not simply say, "Hey, you're supposed to love me regardless of how I take care of myself." When our perspective of bodies is one that is honoring to God as this chapter has discussed, then it is certainly good to take care of them in an effort to remain attractive for our mates. Taking care of ourselves *should* be a priority. For example, have you ever noticed that when some people get divorced and begin to heal from that pain, they suddenly lose weight, change their hair, and start dressing nicer? They do it because they are "on the market" again. It's rational, but it is also hypocritical. If making ourselves as attractive as we can (and I do not mean artificially attractive) while we are dating is a good thing, and if when dating we do it for people that we barely know, then is it not a much greater, even God-honoring, action to keep ourselves as attractive as we can for our mates—the ones we love and have committed to cherish for the rest of our lives?

But, alas, we are not to take our bodies so seriously that we measure their worth by a demeaning cultural standard. Neither are we to measure sexual pleasure by the shape or condition of anything other than our hearts—hearts that offer as a gift to our mate our body and the absolute acceptance of their body; a mutual exchange of donkeys.

THE REAL SUPERMODELS

If your view of beauty is dictated by the cultural idolatry of youth and thinness, you need to repent of believing a lie. Ask God by His grace to change you. Deb, a good friend of mine, was telling her husband about their church's women's retreat, specifically about a conversation she had with four other women, all over the age of fifty. Deb told Buddy, her husband, that these godly women who exuded peace, joy, gentleness, and a deep love for their Savior were absolutely beautiful women. Buddy has been one of my best friends for thirty-five years, and I can hear his exact tone as he said: "Man, you were with the supermodels!"

As those given the privilege of representing the intimacy of Christ and His church in the joy of holy sex, our charge is to see our bodies for what they are: the useful, sturdy, obstinate, and downright funny donkeys described by Saint Francis. And while our bodies are all these, they are also beautiful.

Last year I sat with my friend Buddy on a gulf-view balcony listening to the waves crash on the beaches of the Florida panhandle. The kids were sleeping, and our wives were on their way to join us. Buddy said, "Man, who'da thought? Two south Austin boys marrying so far above their heads. We are blessed."

Smart man, this friend of mine.

QUESTIONS FOR CONVERSATION

1. The statistics cited in this chapter make a strong point about how our culture views the human body. Tell your mate what you learned from this discussion. How has the assault from the culture affected your idea of what represents a "good" body?

2. Discuss the Richard Foster quote: "Conformity to a sick society is to be sick." Do you agree with that statement? Why or why

not? In what ways is our society sick when it comes to the pursuit of beauty?

3. Which ideas from this chapter's discussion of the best ways to view our bodies made the greatest impression on you? Do you agree that we should regard our bodies as useful, but not worthy of adoration—much like we regard a donkey? Do you agree that our obsession with the female breast is culturally created? Identify those ideas in the chapter that caused a reaction in you, good or bad, and discuss those with each other.

4. God calls us to not be conformed to our culture, but to be transformed into the likeness of His Son. That call to not conform to our culture becomes more difficult when leaders within the church teach opposing views. What do you believe about elective cosmetic surgery, a man's assumed "need" to have a physically attractive wife, and the importance of valuing a mate's character over his or her appearance? Share your thoughts with each other.

5. To what degree have you bought into the image of the culture of beauty and thinness? Do you understand why this is contrary to God's perspective? Share with your spouse where you need to grow in this area. Repent of your shortcomings before God and commit to seeing yourself and your mate with the eyes of your loving Creator God. Seek to be a true supermodel according to God's standards.

Chapter 9

Eden Defiled... and Redeemed

A Road Map That Takes Us Back to the Garden

I hate sex!

—A VICTIM OF SEXUAL ABUSE

There is no shortage of jokes about sex. Late-night cable is full of would-be comedians who find the subject of sex to be an easy road to quick laughs. Movies aimed at the teen audience do their part to push "humor" that dehumanizes sex. Girls use food objects to teach their friends how to perform oral sex. Boys masturbate with desserts. And how many times must we see women's breasts used as the consummate distraction for moronic males? These attempts at humor trivialize sex and ridicule people—both of which are creations of God. Trivializing His design and handiwork is anything but holy.

However, in most of these carnival sideshows found on television or in the movies and passed off as entertainment, any difficulty in a character's sex life produces only momentary anguish. A few scenes later the leading man or lady is back in full form, completely recovered from the temporary sexual setback and ready to love another day. The emotional damage is always short-lived in the media, and we're led to believe that this frantic pursuit of sexual fulfillment is, in fact, quite funny. But deep inside we know that such a view is terribly broken. When sex is treated with such disrespect in entertainment and especially in real life, it's no laughing matter.

The amount of emotional, physical, and spiritual pain that is produced by the abuse of God's gift of sex is astounding. It ranges from sex being demeaned in the media to sexual predators getting depraved thrills by victimizing women and children to many forms of unholy sexual practices both within and outside marriage. There's a lot of pain associated with our sexuality, but we must face that pain squarely if we are to fully appreciate God's design for sacred sexuality.

But first let me address a rather common complaint. Many religious skeptics have viewed God as cruel because He put within us an overwhelming desire to have sex then limited its expression to only one person, our mate. However, even a casual look across the landscape of sexual destruction proves that God's intentions for monogamous sex were never cruel, but rather loving and wise. Even if you have never experienced sexual abuse, an extramarital affair, a pornography addiction, or some other sexual trauma, I encourage you to read on. We're all affected by the world around us, by the reality of Eden defiled. Our sexuality is distorted simply because none of us has fully escaped the destructive influences of our culture. As a result, we're all messed up sexually to some extent. We all need insight and perspective as we minister to others—and allow ourselves to be ministered to—in a world where God's creation of sex is badly broken.

A Fire Out of Control

Renowned preacher and educator Haddon Robinson once said that sex and its passions are like fire. Under control, fire serves us by cooking our food and heating our homes. But if you let fire burn out of control, it will destroy everything in its path.[1] It is the nature of this powerful force to do one of two things: to create or to destroy.

Sex has a similar nature. Sexual intimacy within God's boundaries of a loving, committed marriage can provide tremendous joy and fun; it can celebrate intimacy and love; it can bring the blessing of children; and it can create and sustain the mysterious, holy, and sacred oneness of marriage. But if you let it burn outside of God's boundaries, it becomes a self-serving act that can and will destroy careers, marriages, children, reputations, and even life itself. Used well, sex will promote intimacy. Used wrongly, sex will cause division and lead to isolation.

When people who are struggling with their mate's betrayal come to me for counseling, they aren't in my office because of communication problems, financial struggles, a loss of intimacy, or even a "sex problem." They're in pain because they've been utterly betrayed by a spouse who found sexual pleasure elsewhere. They feel as if their heart has been ripped out of their chest. After all, the person with whom they are one has taken the unique symbol of that oneness and broken it. They feel burned—and rightly so. The sacredness of their relationship has been placed on the altar of selfishness and set on fire.

THE LIE OF "JUST SEX"

Our culture tells us that sex need not be taken seriously. A man has an affair and says, "It's nothing personal. It was just sex." College kids practice "hooking up" and say, "It's no big deal. It's just sex." People immerse themselves in pornography and visit strip clubs and say, "Hey, no one was harmed. It's entertainment." The truth is, there is no such thing as sex in a vacuum. Sex always affects relationships, it always affects you, and it always affects your mate. When sexual release is pursued outside of the one-man-one-woman sexual celebration of marriage, then the sacredness of sex is violated. The very heart of this holy union is broken. Sex always has tremendous consequences, either for incredible good or devastating harm.

The highest purpose of sex is to celebrate and re-create oneness between a husband and a wife as we represent Christ and the church. You can't have sex and not establish or damage oneness, no matter who your partner is. This is true even if sexual release is pursued with images of anonymous women in magazines or encounters with nameless chat-room visitors on the Internet. Fantasy sex is a violation of the oneness you share with your mate. Every sexual encounter affects its participants, even if that encounter involves only one person gazing at an image on a video screen.

Addressing the Christians who lived in Corinth, the apostle Paul confronted the pagan ritual practice of having sex with temple prostitutes. In referencing Genesis 2:24, Paul asked, "Do you not know that he who unites himself with a prostitute is one with her in body? For it is said, 'The two will become one flesh'" (1 Corinthians 6:16). Engaging sexually with another person, even with a prostitute where there is no apparent emotional involvement, is still not "just sex." Since God designed sex to produce oneness, the bond that sex forms can't be separated from the act no matter how desecrated that act may become.

Sex between a committed, Christ-focused husband and wife creates and celebrates passion and intimacy. Sex between two strangers, autoerotic sex stimulated by pornography, and even sex between those who love each other but are not married—all this creates division, hurt, and a sense of betrayal. It's not "just sex." It's a soul-damaging experience.

PARADISE DEFILED

Paradise on earth was defiled when Adam and Eve chose to disobey God. In essence, their sin was that, despite His abundant provision for all their needs, they no longer wanted to trust God to do what was best for them. When Adam was sinless and yet still lonely, God not only provided for that need, but He did so in the best possible way with the gift of Eve. Adam and Eve both needed to feel that someone knew them deeply and loved them anyway. That need was met by God's graciously giving them the celebration of holy sex. Then, however, confronted with the opportunity to trust themselves for what was best, they took it. They failed to trust God's words to them, and they wanted to obtain His ability to discern right from wrong, good from evil. They no longer felt that God knew best, and pain and destruction followed.

The desire to be loved and needed by another human being, the hunger to know that our life matters to someone else, is a God-given need. It's as universal as our hunger to know God. After all, He designed us to be in relationship with Him and in fellowship with others. Our Father wants us to know both that our lives matter to Him and that He has provided the pathway to fulfill the longing of our souls through a relationship with His Son. He also supplied the answer to our human loneliness, through marriage and sexual intimacy for those who enter into marriage, and through the fellowship of believers for those who remain single.

We can choose to remove God from the picture, but our need for love and intimacy still remains. Without God to guide us and provide for those desires, we confuse sex with love. We long to be loved, we long to know that we matter to someone else, and something tells us that engaging in sex will accomplish what we want. So, attempting to find our own solution to what will fill this hole in our hearts, we engage in sex outside of God's boundaries. And pain and destruction follow.

LOOKING FOR LOVE

Jenna was a thirty-year-old single mom overwhelmed by loneliness. She was an attractive woman with a delightful laugh. But one look at Jenna told me she was following the wrong path to fill the emotional void in her life. Everything about the way she dressed and presented herself testified to the fact that she saw herself as a sex object. Her tight, revealing clothing attracted plenty of attention wherever she went.

Jenna was just nine years old when her grandfather began to abuse her sexually. When her parents were away from home, he'd take her upstairs, have her undress, and then use her for his sexual pleasure. During the whole encounter and especially afterward, the grandfather would say, "I love you, Jenna. I love you so much."

The abuse continued for more than two years, and by the time Jenna entered puberty she had formed a self-defeating connection in her mind that equated sex with love. When she was thirteen, she was asked out by a fifteen-year-old boy. Because of her mind-set, their date to the barn for her first experience of consensual intercourse seemed perfectly natural. For the next eighteen months, she'd sneak out of her house to the barn whenever the boy called. It was always the same—a few minutes of talk, a few minutes of sex, and he'd leave. Jenna was occasionally bothered by the fact that this same boy ignored her at school. She'd soon get over that, however, the next time they had sex and he said, "I love you, Jenna."

As a teenager, Jenna had sex with dozens of boys. It was the only way that she felt loved. At age twenty-four, she got pregnant and married Greg, a guy whose view of sex had nothing to do with love. For Greg, sex was a physiological urge that required regular attention—as demonstrated by his frequent affairs. Fearing that she would lose him, Jenna pursued sex with Greg more often. She believed that as long as Greg still had sex with her, he still loved her.

For the next two years, Jenna struggled to be a good wife and mom, desperately wanting her husband to love her. All the while Greg visited topless clubs, watched porno movies, and indulged in sex magazines. They continued to have sex regularly, but whatever tenderness there had been waned dramatically. When the "I love you"s ended, Jenna's link between sex and love ended—at least with Greg. Deciding there must be someone who would love her, she ended the marriage, but she didn't end her confusion. Now, four years later, after a long string of casual sex partners, Jenna was as lonely as ever.

Jenna's story epitomizes the epidemic of sex/love confusion in our culture. Not everybody's story will be as painful as this one. But all who pursue sex apart from a true knowledge and experience of love, and all who chase after it for the sole purpose of self-satisfaction, will find themselves in the same wilderness Jenna was in. Needing to feel loved, these lost souls will pursue sexual activity but find only momentary relief from their loneliness. The more they look to sex for the answer, the farther they'll wander into the desert, away from the Promised Land and away from the beauty and fulfillment that sex is meant to provide. At that point, Eden has been defiled almost beyond recognition.

Sex Can Destroy

As we noted earlier, the things that have the greatest potential for good also possess the ability for tremendous destruction if they're misused. Sex tops the list of good things that have been misused to the destruction of countless lives. To help us understand the consequences of violating God's design for holy sex, let's look at the four horsemen of sexual degradation.

The Horseman of Sexual Abuse

Those who have endured the trauma of sexual abuse have suffered a psychological earthquake. Something special was taken from them that they didn't freely choose to give. And since that "something" is sexual, the impact goes from the emotional frustration of being robbed all the way to feeling as if your soul itself has been raped. God connected our soul (the vital existence of mind, body, and spirit together) and our sexuality (that which is holy and which mysteriously represents Christ and His bride, the church). When our bodies are sexually violated, our minds and our spirits are violated as well.

As a result, many dear people have been robbed of their ability to give themselves freely in the experience of holy sexuality. Even someone who is hypersexual, as we saw with Jenna, isn't giving herself freely to the holy mystery of a sexual celebration. Instead of seeking spiritual oneness with a mate, she is giving herself to others sexually out of compulsion. Hers is a driven—and empty—attempt to find love through sexual expression.

The other common response of someone who has been sexually abused is the direct opposite: Instead of pursuing sex in a desperate attempt to find love, this person tries to avoid things sexual altogether. To survive a sexual encounter, even in marriage, they feel they must give their bodies but transport their minds and their hearts to a safe place, far from the sexual event. Every sexual encounter can be a reminder of the abuse. Like Jenna, these people want to matter deeply to another person. But in trying to solve the puzzle of sex and intimacy, they can't help but still equate sex and intimacy with pain. Their innate desire to be known and loved, to be naked and unashamed, is overwhelmed by the pain. They are unable to share their hopes and dreams, their fears and hurts, or even spiritual intimacy with their mates because it all equals, in their minds, letting someone get close enough to hurt them again.

The Horseman of Pornography

It has been said that a man seeking to satisfy his sexual cravings with pornography is like a man dying of thirst lusting after salt.[2] As an addiction, pornography accelerates the law of diminishing returns. There's always the hope of finally finding satisfaction and fulfillment with the next pornographic encounter. The lie of pornography is that lasting sexual satisfaction will be had with the next event. You feel that since you were satisfied for a moment or two, you just need a little bit more. Walking the path of pornography is like filling a bathtub with water, floating a little plastic ball on top, and then opening the drain. You may not notice the ball move too much at first, but as the water level drops, the ball will get closer and closer to the bottom, eventually caught in a whirlpool where it has no choice but to get sucked down to the sewer. Pornography will always pull you and your marriage toward the sewer.

The sexual allure of pornography is not simply about nudity. If that were the sole attraction, anyone who views pornography would only need one magazine or one Web site displaying nude images. But that one image of one nude woman doesn't satisfy. So new materials are being produced at an alarming rate, not just to display naked bodies, but to feed the fantasy that goes with those images. Men who have become conditioned to visual stimulation confuse the "come hither" look of the nude model with someone who longs to be with them. Pornography users ignore the truth that, if the woman in the picture sat next to them on a plane, she wouldn't give them the time of day. Furthermore, a picture of one nude woman will provide stimulation for a while, but without a relationship and true intimacy, there can't be lasting fulfillment. It's impossible. So the porn user always needs yet another picture of yet another woman looking at him with seeming desire.

The test of appropriate, God-honoring sexual behavior is this: "Does it promote oneness with my spouse?" The answer with pornography is "Absolutely not." It's amazing that some counselors and therapists encourage couples to "spice up their sex lives" with pornography, which only serves to drive couples farther from any promise of true intimacy. You can't be emotionally one with your mate and indulge in pornography. It's fire and water; the two don't mix. And in this case, with pornography as the fire, all will be destroyed.

Consider the situation from the standpoint of a wife who catches her husband viewing pornography. She objects strenuously, and he counters with, "It's not like I had an affair." But the reality is that he did have an affair. His viewing of pornography, even occasionally, tells his wife that she's not enough. She understandably concludes that her husband chose to find fulfillment and excitement somewhere else because he somehow found her inadequate. Any move away from marital intimacy is movement away from your mate—and your God.

The Horseman of "Casual" Sex

If there is a word that totally contradicts the idea of God-honoring sex, that word is *casual*. Sex that is sacred is never casual. It's always careful, disciplined, and deliberate. The parameters God has given us for the expression of our sexuality prohibit thoughtless sex. But our culture hasn't caught on to that truth.

Consider the sexual fad of "hooking up" among teenagers and college students. Hooking up refers to the practice of getting together with someone for the sole purpose of having sex. It is consensual, there is no pretense of affection for the other person, and there's no expectation of any future relationship. It's almost unbelievable in this day of AIDS and the scores of other sexually transmitted diseases. Yet, in other respects, it's not surprising at all. It's another consequence of the separation of sex from marriage, intimacy, and holiness. The concepts of sex and relationship, of sex and lifelong commitment, are no longer linked in most people's minds.

Without people's awareness of the ultimate purposes of sexual intimacy, and with the loss of the knowledge that those purposes can be achieved only within the lovingly created boundaries of marriage, there is no need for limitations on sexual expression because there's nothing left to keep penned up. If there is no ultimate, God-ordained purpose for sex, then all things are not only permissible, they're desirable. Even the willing engagement in sex with someone you hope to never see again.

The Horseman of Broken Promises

In a culture that constantly feeds us lies about sex, the idea that sex will be more fun with someone other than my mate is easy to believe. Reliable statistics for the number of people who actually carry on extramarital affairs are hard to come by. (Studies show a range spanning from 10 to 50 percent.) More important than "how many," however, is "why?" Why do men and women choose to have sex with someone other than the one to whom they promised to be faithful?

I don't want to oversimplify the matter. It can sometimes take numerous counseling sessions to discover all the factors leading up to infidelity, with some causes buried deep in a person's past. The behavior can be born out of boredom, unrealistic expectations, loneliness, sexual addictions, emotional immaturity, a felt need to punish self or others, or a desire to exit the relationship. I would make the case, however, that all of those circumstances—including traumas from the past—have in common a high degree of confusion over love, sex, and intimacy.

A man feeling isolated from his wife after the birth of a child may have an affair in the belief that the sexual encounter will make him feel desired and needed—it doesn't. A woman may end up in bed with a man who shows her love and attention when she hasn't felt that from her husband. She believes that she loves the other man, that he loves her, and that sex will bring them closer. It does—for a short while, and then she is empty again. Or a man or woman may feel "out of love" with their mate; they believe the attraction is gone. They meet someone who doesn't exhibit any of their spouse's flaws. This other person is always courteous, always attentive, always available, and never critical. "Sex with them will be the sex I am looking for!" And it is—for a while.

People enter into all avenues of extramarital sex with the belief that they've been missing out on something that a different sex partner will provide. Regardless of the circumstances or the activity, even if there is a short-lived sense of fulfillment, the affair will ultimately leave the person feeling that there is *still* something missing. The myth always explodes. An affair always ravages a marriage like a neutron bomb. The house may be left standing, but all life inside it seems as if it has been wiped off the map.

All four of these horsemen are spurred on by the separation of sex from love, from intimacy, from marriage, and from God. Broken lives, broken hearts, broken marriages, and even broken spirits are left in their wake. Some people, like those who were sexually abused, have been forcibly robbed. Some, like those who engage in "casual" sex, have been duped by a world that reduces sex to the level of a simple biological function. Others have asked to be robbed by choosing to travel the path of pornography or by breaking their promise through adultery.

And all of these people are hurting; all of them are looking for answers. And the loving God who provided the gift of love and sex in the first place is also the only One who can provide ultimate hope. However, instead of turning to Him first, many have turned to the wisdom of mankind, including the hope offered by medical science. Doctors, by training, often look for a physical cause behind what seems to be a physical problem. When sex is viewed primarily as a biological function, medication might seem to be the most promising solution. But as we look at the ways Eden has been defiled, we need to remember that sex is not primarily a biological function. It's about holiness, intimacy, mystery, and oneness. If the awareness of those elements is missing, then it's very possible, even probable, that the prescribed medical solution will fail. Instead, an approach that unites sex, intimacy, passion, and holiness often will eliminate the physical dysfunction.

How Eden Is Redeemed

For some of you, sex may be a horrible reminder of a devastating event or series of events from your past—or even your present. You don't see how sex could ever be anything sacred or holy. For you, it has produced nothing but pain. I want you to know that people once felt that way about the cross, too. Two thousand years ago, the cross was a symbol of unimaginable pain and public shame. It represented death; it was a sign of the finality of the grave. But then God sent Jesus to earth, and today the cross hangs in the vast majority of Christian churches in the world. Although for some people a cross may simply be meaningless jewelry, for believers it is the sign of our hope. What once was a symbol of shame and death is now a symbol of God's grace, God's power, and God's ability to bring life to what once was dead.

Paul wrote, "When you were dead in your sins and in the uncircumcision of your sinful nature, God made you alive with Christ. He forgave us all our sins, having canceled the written code, with its regulations, that was against us and that stood opposed to us; he took it away, nailing it to the cross" (Colossians 2:13-14). Jesus Christ has conquered the death of the cross and brought us life; and He can bring to life what is dead in your life as well. And that means that He is able to redeem and heal your view and experience of sex. Today, this side of the Resurrection, the cross represents the unconditional love and acceptance of a grace-filled God; today, sex can, because of the cross, represent the unconditional love and acceptance of a mate celebrated in a holy gift of God's grace. Let's take a look at how God's grace specifically defeats the four horsemen of sexual degradation.

Grace for the Sexually Abused

The cross is the answer, the solution, and the healing for those who have been victimized by sexual abuse. Yet I can't explain why some people can earnestly pray for God's healing in the area of sexual brokenness and receive it quickly, while others seem to pray and search, and the pain remains. But I do know that the answer, regardless, is the cross. The only way the gift of holy sexuality can be redeemed for someone who has suffered sexually at the hands of another is through the cross of Christ. For those of you who live in this pain, I encourage you to find competent, caring, Christian help. In addition, find a group of people you can share your pain with who will pray for you and love you. There is help—and God does want you to be healed.

God wants you to experience the joy of giving yourself freely to your mate in holy sexuality. I've had clients who, out of fear and pain, have asked why they just can't let their mates have sex with them while their minds are somewhere else. They don't want to fight through the pain. The answer is that if they stay as they are, they are missing out on a wonderful experience that God has for them. They can choose not to return to Eden, but in so doing they miss the joy of God's plan for holy sexuality and thus fail to enter the Promised Land of marriage.

Grace in the Pornography Battle

If you struggle with pornography, the first step is to admit it. You need to realize and acknowledge that there is no such thing as a "little harmless pornography." I've had numerous clients whose addiction to pornography began as a curious venture onto a Web site or by watching an in-room movie during a business trip. Later they sit weeping in my office, having been discovered after months and months of new Web sites and new movies. Whether you've merely dabbled or have a serious addiction, you must seek help—including help from your mate. Husbands and wives who desire to create a marriage that fully enters into the mystery of holy sex must fight together against the deadly intrusion of pornography, and they must fight in prayer and with love. Help is available, and it's as near as the cross.

With prayer, accountability, and the power of God, pornography addiction can be overcome. The temptation lurks each time you log on to your computer, walk past a newsstand, or check into a hotel by yourself. To resist the temptation, build accountability into your life and realize fully just how such an unholy venue pollutes the holiness God desires for our marriages.

As we discussed earlier, one of the great lies of pornography is that it's harmless since it happens alone. The truth is, pornography harms you, your mate, and the holiness of your oneness. One of the most effective ways to battle it is to seek the help of a support partner. I nearly always encourage a man who is struggling with pornography to bring his wife in on the battle. I know how frightening that sounds, especially in light of my earlier discussion on the effects that a husband's involvement in pornography can have on a wife. However, as your wife desires *with* you to achieve and maintain sexual holiness, she is in a better position to battle with you against this enemy than anyone else you know. She is your partner in the journey back to Eden. She wants to join with you in the endeavor of oneness. Since she is your ally, let her be the warrior by your side.

Male accountability is also a useful weapon. If you travel, you will find it incredibly helpful to have a brother in Christ ask you about your trip. If you're tempted to watch that in-room movie, give this brother a call from the road. You need someone who will encourage you, pray for you, and ask you the tough questions. Be bold and approach a friend. It won't be difficult to find other men who share your struggle.

Grace for Those Who Pursued "Casual Sex"

God is not out to spoil our fun. Within the boundaries for holy sex that He has established, He is, instead, protecting our ultimate sexual enjoyment. Those boundaries are there to protect its highest and best good. If you've found yourself violating these boundaries, then turn around. The trail you're on will never give you what you're looking for. Only within God's system will you ever experience the completion your soul desires. Casual sex is by definition meaningless sex. It's a misdirected attempt to solve loneliness or to seek wholeness. It will always leave you empty. But sex with an understanding of its true meaning and experienced within God's boundaries will leave you fulfilled and feeling loved. The contrast between the two couldn't be more dramatic.

For those who are unmarried, I encourage you to wait. You might be convinced that if you abstain from sex, you'll be missing out. Missing out on momentary pleasure, yes. Missing out on what God intends sex to be? No. And by waiting, you'll also miss out on all the collateral damage that comes from crossing the boundaries. All sexual activity outside God's design damages your life. I have yet to meet a couple who has said, "You know, I'm *so* glad we slept around before we got married." I haven't even had a couple tell me, "We're glad we slept with each other before we got married. We have no regrets." But I've had many talk at length about their regret, their pain, and the damage that having sex outside God's parameters caused them. Even if it's not a case of promiscuity, sex before marriage is damaging. Always.

For all of you who are hurting, take hope. God is in the mending business. Let Him mend the fences that you have broken down in the past. Ask Him to mend your heart from the pain it has endured. Know that healing is found in the cross. Trust His design for holy sex to bring you the sense of wholeness, joy, and fulfillment that come only through oneness with your mate.

Grace for Those Who Broke Their Promises

Although it may seem unlikely or even impossible to you, God can heal your marriage from the damage and betrayal of an affair. This healing, however, usually requires outside help not only from God, but also from others who can help you understand why the betrayal happened and then guide you into the kind of marriage relationship that can keep it from happening again. I'm not saying God isn't enough, but this is one of the many situations where God's love, wisdom, and grace often are dispensed through the hands of His children.

Also, if you ever feel tempted to pursue an affair, ask God to help you destroy the lies that promise a shortcut to better sex and see the true destruction that it will bring. Speak to friends, speak to your pastor, speak to God. And then set your mind and heart on pursuing love and marriage from a commitment to love and obey God. Pray to understand the power of loving commitment. The cross cannot only heal pain from the past, it can also give you strength to prevent the pain that may lie ahead.

So if you earnestly desire to experience marriage, including holy sexual intimacy, the way God designed, you must ruthlessly fight together with your spouse to keep Eden from being defiled in your relationship. You must also let God ruthlessly fight to redeem what has been damaged. In every moment of sexual temptation or weakness, ask yourself the two core questions of marital intimacy:

- Will this promote oneness with my mate?
- Is it my mate and my mate alone who is giving me sexual excitement?

With God's help, you must build fences that protect holy sex. Do not share intimacies, even in conversation, that should only be shared with your mate. Don't flirt, create emotional connections, or fantasize about anyone other than your spouse. Remember, you've made your selection and the menu is closed.

Finally, after taking such a detailed look at how Eden is defiled, some of you may doubt that the cross provides a complete solution. Depending on your background and circumstances, you may need to seek the help of a qualified Christian counselor as well as the accountability of your mate and trusted friends. But if you are asking, "Is the cross of Christ enough?" the answer is always and resoundingly yes. The grace of God that took the cross from being an icon of despair to a symbol of hope is the same grace that can take sex from being a source of confusion and pain to being an experience of love, holiness, and worship.

Through the cross of Christ, you and your mate can live in purity and joy. You can experience the mystery of being naked and unashamed. Together, you can return to the garden by celebrating the true presence of God through the gift of oneness. Through the hope of the cross, Eden has been redeemed.

The cross is enough—and it's the only thing that is.

QUESTIONS FOR CONVERSATION

1. Share with each other your thoughts on the idea that sex is never "just sex." Do you agree with this view? Why or why not?

2. Even if you may have been spared any damaging effects from the four horsemen mentioned in this chapter, you are still affected by living in a culture that demeans and misuses sex. Discuss with your mate how living in a culture that defiles Eden has shaped your beliefs about sex. Do you struggle with the idea that sex can be holy in the midst of all the degradation? Pray together for God to change your eyes—and the world.

3. If you have suffered any of the sexual violations discussed in this chapter, your healing is found in the grace and love of God and in the grace and love of your mate. Talk to your mate about your pain; seek his or her support, help, and, most of all, love and prayers. If necessary, find a competent Christ-centered counselor who can help you.

4. Where are you right now on your journey to the Promised Land? Consider together whether you're just now approaching that territory, whether you have recently crossed over and are enjoying the milk and honey, or whether you're still in the desert. In light of the discussion of God's healing through the cross, where do you think God wants you to be? What will you do to get there? Make a specific plan—together.

5. Spend time together praying. Ask God for His healing in your own life and in the lives of others who need His special touch. Tell each other, again and again, how much you love each other and are committed to each other. And tell each other, again and again, that the cross is enough—and that it is the only thing that is.

Chapter 10

The Covenant of Marriage

The One Thing You Do Have Control Over

Anyone who thinks marriage is a fifty-fifty proposition doesn't understand women or fractions.

—Danny Thomas

Now that we've explored the Promised Land of fulfilling, holy sex, you may be thinking: *Who in their right mind wouldn't want to dwell in that sacred territory?* I've spoken to many people, in large groups as well as one on one in my office, about God's design for holy sex, and most of them know immediately that this is what they're looking for. Still, it seems that very few couples actually find their way to that place of joy, intimacy, and oneness.

If God's Promised Land of sexual blessing is such a sought-after destination, why do so few people find it? To answer that, let me ask a second question: If there's anything you could do to make your spouse's life easier or more fulfilling, and if there's anything you could do to make your mate feel more loved, more cherished, and more valued, why do you hesitate to do those things?

That's a tough one to answer. Some would claim they don't go along with their mate's preferences because doing so would involve submitting to unreasonable requests, immoral actions, or behaviors that violate their conscience. Fair enough, so let's bypass anything that would fall within those categories. We'll also exclude any actions that could create some sort of jeopardy. For instance, you know that a morning liaison would please your mate, but it would also make you late to work and threaten your job security. Or let's say your spouse would love to take a romantic seven-day cruise, but it's not in the budget and would imperil your family's financial stability. Or you could be fun loving and uninhibited and run naked through the rain, but you already have the flu and you'd be asking for pneumonia. (Okay, I stretched on that one.)

Now that we've taken care of the exceptions, let's get back to the question: Why wouldn't we do anything we knew would make our mates feel loved? Well, to start with, we're busy and we're tired. And sometimes we don't feel well. And then there's all this work to catch up on, and we have our own needs to take care of, and the laundry's piling up, and the bills need to be paid, and... Those are common excuses, but they fail to answer the question. At its root, any attempt to justify not choosing loving actions toward our mates is an argument rooted in selfishness. Love, from God's perspective, is always about doing, not just about feeling. Love is about commitment and the choices we make. It's about deciding not to be selfish.

"Hold on!" you say. "You don't know *my* mate. You wouldn't *believe* what he or she did the other day!" Sorry, that argument doesn't hold water either. Any attempt to define love in the context of what the other person does or doesn't do violates God's definition of love as well as the vows you spoke on your wedding day. In Ephesians 5:25, husbands are told to love their wives, period; in 1 Corinthians 13, Paul tells us that love is patient, kind, not rude, not self-seeking, and more. Nowhere in these places or any other places in the New Testament will you find the fulfillment of God's command to love our mate based on anything they do. Your words and your actions the day you got married stated before God that you would forever cherish this one you were committing yourself to and that you would guard this oneness that God was about to create.

And you thought you were nervous on your wedding day because you were going to move in with someone who might put the toilet paper roll on backward.

BACK TO THE BEGINNING

If your wedding vows bore any resemblance to the traditional ones, you'll recall that the words "as long as we both feel like it" weren't used. Unless you were married by a justice of the peace, your vows contained words of lifelong, unconditional commitment. You spoke words of a *verba solemnia,* a solemn vow. But when you made that declaration, were you forming a covenant or entering into a contractual arrangement?

Sometimes I feel as if we Americans are drowning in contracts. Whether we need an auto loan, a raise at work, or a driver's license, we're constantly putting our name on the dotted line. A contract is an arrangement between two parties whereby both sides commit to certain conditions. Inherent in the agreement is the idea that if one side violates the terms, the other party has some type of recourse. If you don't pay back the money you owe, the bank is free to repossess your car. If you're ticketed too many times for speeding, the judge will suspend your driving privileges. The provisions in a contract protect the interests of both parties.

Contrast that with what happens in a wedding ceremony. Most couples seem to believe that, since both the man and the woman are asked to speak the marriage vows, they have established a contract. In one partner's mind, that means he'll do his part as long as his spouse is doing her part. "I'll speak kindly to you as long as you speak kindly to me. I'll have sex with you as long as you meet all of my emotional needs." A contractual arrangement is designed to protect one person's interests in the event the other party fails to fulfill his or her obligations.

Almost weekly in my office, I see evidence of this perspective on wedding vows. It's rare when a husband kicks things off by saying, "My wife is wonderful. She's the most giving, unselfish, loving woman in the world. But I've really messed up. I guess I'm just a jerk." When a couple comes in for counseling, the conversation is more like this:

Ed: "Well, it's like this. Marge won't have sex with me even though I haven't as much as flirted with any other woman as long as we've been married."

Marge: "Well, I'd be more likely to have sex with him if he'd lift a finger around the house. He expects me to keep things clean and the kids taken care of even though I spend more hours at work than he does."

Ed: "Oh, my heart is breaking! She begged me to buy her a bigger house, knowing full well it would mean that we'd both have to work overtime. Now all I get is nag, nag, nag."

And on it goes. Each spouse recites a long litany of the other person's failure to fulfill the terms of the supposed contract. I regularly remind couples that neither of them signed a contract that gives them an out if their mate fails to perform up to standards. What they entered into on their wedding day was a covenant. And the terms of a covenant bear very little similarity to those of a contract. Understanding what you actually agreed to on your wedding day, and why God wants you to live out what you committed to, is the only way to enter the Promised Land of holy sex.

GROUNDS FOR A COVENANT

A covenant is an agreement made by choice, it's an agreement made by commitment, and it's an agreement that is in no way dependent upon what the other party does. Within the requirements of a covenant agreement, you don't have the option of loving and cherishing your mate only as long as he or she loves and cherishes you. There is no quid pro quo.

Gordon Hugenberger, professor of Old Testament at Gordon-Conwell Theological Seminary, provides a helpful study of the scriptural concept of covenant. The predominant sense of the Old Testament Hebrew word for covenant is "an elected, as opposed to natural, relationship of obligation established under divine sanction."[1] It's a relationship you choose to enter into, and by entering this relationship you make the commitment to meet the terms of the covenant. Unlike a purely human arrangement, a covenant is authorized by God, supported by God, and ratified by God.

Hugenberger further explains that covenants always have a relational aspect and carry a primary "obligation of love." This is why marriage and adoption provide the models and the subsequent formula for all theological covenants of the Old Testament.[2] In adoption, you choose your child without the natural obligation created by being a birth parent. You commit to nurturing and caring for the child regardless of what the baby gives you in return. Likewise, God chose to adopt us as His children, making it possible through Christ, and He has committed Himself to care for us by His grace and through the gift of the Holy Spirit. In Christ, God established a covenant with us.

The formula for establishing a covenant has two parts: (1) a ratifying oath, which would be the spoken words, and (2) an oath sign, a symbolic and specific action that would seal the deal.[3] A vivid example of our covenant-making God in action is when He said to Noah, "Never again will all life be cut off by the waters of a flood," and then put a rainbow in the sky as "the sign of the covenant" (see Genesis 9:11-13).

The ratifying oath we speak during the wedding ceremony is our solemn vow before God and our soon-to-be spouse. These words are solemn, Hugenberger writes, "because they are uttered before the deity."[4]

"Bone of my bones and flesh of my flesh" was the *verba solemnia* spoken by Adam[5] (Genesis 2:23). Our wedding vows are made in the presence of God Himself.

After we have made our solemn vow of love and loyalty, God then calls us to do something even more solemn to finalize the covenant of marriage. It's an action that celebrates and represents God's holy presence. By now, what the oath sign is should come as no surprise. The oath sign that seals the deal of marriage is nothing less than the act of sacred sex.

SEALED WITH A WHAT?

Since marriage has always been defined by God as two becoming one, the sexual union of a wife and husband is the perfect, God-intended oath sign that a marriage has been established. We speak an oath with our vows; we seal that oath with our bodies. Together, our words and our action form a covenant. And once again we see why God so forcefully opposes sex outside marriage. It's not because He is a kill-joy Creator who goes out of His way to steal all our fun, but rather because He created sexual intimacy to be so much more than self-pleasure. Sex is not only part of the covenant of marriage, but it functions in the *creation* of the covenant. Sex is the divine seal.

Moreover, sexual intercourse reestablishes the covenant each time it is celebrated, just as oneness and the mystery of Christ are proclaimed each time we join ourselves intimately with our mate. Our coming together as wife and husband, the two becoming one in order to jointly represent God's divine image, is to be a regular reminder of the promises we made in our marriage covenant, just as a rainbow is to be a reminder of God's promise in His covenant with Noah after the flood.

This covenant theology of marriage and sex ties together everything we've been discussing: the holiness of sex, the mystery of sexual oneness, and the worship that happens when we acknowledge God's presence during our intimate celebration. All these aspects of sacred sex are protected by this elected relationship of obligation. The marriage covenant is what drives us toward each other in times of joy and in times of sadness. It's what causes us to ache to be with each other when we're apart. And it's why couples at a point of deep emotional crisis—such as an unexpected death, the revelation of a pending divorce between friends, or the disclosure of a sexual betrayal in a marriage you thought "it could never happen to"—often express to their mate, "I need to feel you inside me." Each time we enter into the holy act of sex, we again pronounce our solemn declaration: "I do. I still do."

THE MARRIAGE MARATHON

I'm convinced that anybody with two healthy legs could run a marathon— if that person commits to training for it. Now I didn't say that everybody could complete the race with a world-class time. But with the commitment to run the twenty-six-plus miles, people can indeed cross the finish line.

When I started martial arts training with my sons, the rank of black belt that I now hold seemed a long way off—especially for my then-unlimber thirty-seven-year-old body. But as I have watched people come and go from our school, some making it to black belt and others quitting along the way, I've observed that those who attain that coveted rank don't do so because they're more talented, more athletic, or just plain lucky. They attain this level because they are committed to training. And training, as our martial arts instructor says, is about discipline, respect, and perfecting the basics.

I'm convinced that any of us married couples can have a great marriage and an intimate, soul-touching sex life if we will commit to training. This training will lead us to be disciplined in the behaviors God calls us to as married believers, it will cause us to respect our mates, and it will challenge us to work hard on perfecting the basics. We'll base all we say and do on our faith in God and our desire to fulfill the duties of the covenant we've established. The first thing we need is commitment.

But we live in a culture that doesn't like commitment. Health club membership, cellular phone service, and various leases are now available on a month-to-month basis—"No long-term commitment required." Magazines offer trial subscriptions. And the ethos of low- or no-commitment has affected marriage as well. People say, "I don't see any point in being committed to the institution of marriage when I'm no longer in love with my mate. That would be stupid." But we are not called to commit to the thing called marriage; God calls us to commit to following Him, to loving our mates, and to living out the holy mystery of marriage on a daily basis.

As believers, our commitment in marriage begins on that day of our vows. But according to counselor and marital researcher Scott Stanley, our commitment "is not about staying together; it's about being together in the full mystery of marriage."[6] Who can fully articulate the reasons why the touch of one we care so much about can bring peace and alleviate fears? Who can explain the pain we experience simply because our mates are in pain, we are separated from them, or worse, we have caused their hurt? Who on this earth can prove why God-honoring sexual oneness can fill voids in our life? Only God can answer these questions. It's part of the mystery.

And it's that mystery that we commit to living out with our mates. It is in the mystery of marriage that we experience healing from our God-created loneliness. Jesus tells a story of woman who so longed for the emptiness of her life to be filled, and yet she was committed not to the mystery but to simply being with men. Author Ken Gire reflects on the encounter between Jesus and a person we know only as "the woman at the well." In this brief encounter detailed in John 4, we learn that this Samaritan woman (a mixed race of half-Jews normally despised by Jews) has been married five times and is currently living with a man who is not legally her husband. She is coming to draw water when Christ offers her "living water" that will finally quench the spiritual thirst that has plagued her for so long. Gire writes, "She has gone from man to man like one lost in the desert, sun-struck and delirious. For her, marriage has been a retreating mirage. Again and again she's returned to the matrimonial well, hoping to draw some-thing from it to quench her thirst for love and happiness, but again and again she has left that well, disappointed."[7]

This woman is longing to be loved, yearning to be fulfilled. Something tells her that marriage is the answer, and each failed relationship only leaves her looking for the next hope of completion. But every time she comes up empty. Pastor M. Craig Barnes writes, "This craving to fill life's empty places forms the cosmic axis around which our world turns. No matter where the search leads us—through one relationship after another, through job after job, into therapy, recreation, and achievements, and even through different churches—we continue to believe this next thing will fulfill us. That is our sacred hope."[8]

To enter the Promised Land of marital and sexual fulfillment, we must commit to live in the midst of two mysteries. First is the mystery of salva-tion, our relationship with God through His Son, Jesus Christ. This rela-tionship is the only source of genuine and ultimate fulfillment. It is, for believers, lived out through the mystery of Christ who has made both Jews and Gentiles into one church and who has provided for us the undeserved entry into the Holy of Holies, which is the very presence of God Himself. Second is the mystery of marriage. We must fully understand that elimi-nating the void of loneliness that God created marriage to fill does *not* hap-pen by demanding that our mate do anything. Rather, we must come to the matrimonial well determined to *put water into it ourselves*. To be com-mitted to living within this mystery means that we entrust ourselves to

God as we obligate ourselves to serve our spouse. As we serve our spouse, we are finally fulfilled. And again, this mystery is fulfilled through commitment.

A Tale of Two Commitments

Fulfilling the covenant of marriage requires two practical aspects of living out our daily commitment. Marital researchers have called these "constraint commitment" and "dedication commitment."

Constraint commitment creates a sense of obligation, the realization that there would be heavy costs if you abandoned the commitment. Joining the military is a good example. If you're in the first year of a three-year commitment to the marines and find yourself pulling guard duty at an outpost in Iceland, your superior officers would take a dim view of your leaving just because you decided you'd prefer to be stationed in the Bahamas. There is a constraint (like the brig) that keeps you shivering in Iceland.

Dedication commitment, on the other hand, stems from your sense of internal devotion and the realization that you're moving forward along a path that leads to a desired destination. Being able to suffer though your sophomore literature class is doable because you keep your eyes on the goal of a college degree and what it will bring you (my apologies to literature majors). You're dedicated, committed to hanging in there through the good times and bad, because you're keeping your eyes on the prize.

Research shows that couples who act out of both constraint and dedication commitment not only have marriages that last, but marriages that are also happier, more intimate, and more fulfilled.[9] These couples realize that God's boundaries have constrained them, but those constraints aren't seen as a prison sentence. Instead, just as God's boundaries for sexual expression maximize the experience, so too do God's protective boundaries of marital commitment maximize that experience. Constraint provides protection.

But we're not just protected from the pain of an affair or the devastation of divorce. Constraint also creates intimacy and trust. For example, Amy and I committed before we were married that we'd never use the word *divorce* in any argument or as a threat, no matter how angry or hurt or hopeless we felt. I've counseled too many couples who were devastated when "that word" was thrown out in the heat of an argument—and years later, it still hasn't been forgotten. Both spouses know that, at one time, at least one of them seriously considered surrendering. Constraint commitment erases such doubt, giving you the comfort that even when one of you is acting like a jerk (that would be me), your mate will still be there. It's a boundary of protection against surrender when the battle turns ugly.

Dedication commitment, on the other hand, is much more proactive. It's about actively fulfilling the vows of our covenant; it's about serving our mates in the way God directs. It's about making them feel as if they're the most important person in the world to us every day of our lives. In short, it's all about choices.

CHOOSE THE RIGHT THING

When you bring a child home from the hospital, you've made a commitment to love her, feed her, and keep her safe (and feed her some more). I have yet to meet the mom of a newborn who told me that, at three in the morning, at the first peep of her baby, she springs out of bed wide-eyed and smiling, sore nipples and all, singing "Happy Days Are Here Again!" And yet, when the child is hungry in the middle of the night, moms and dads all over the world, with breast or bottle, feed their babies. They don't do it because they feel like it; they do it because it's the right thing to do. They do it out of love, and they do it out of commitment.

God has given all of us this ability to choose to do the right thing even when we don't feel like it. That ability is key because at the heart of our commitments to our mates is the realization that we have choices. And at the heart of experiencing holy sex is the realization that we have choices. No matter what our mates say to us, we can speak kindly to them; no matter what promise they fail to carry through on, we can still be nice to them; and no matter what hurtful thing they do, we can forgive them. It's a matter of choice.

One of the most widely accepted lies of our day is this one: "You make me so angry!" The truth is that I may not like what you do; I may think your actions or words are offensive. But if I get angry as a result, I can't blame anyone else for my response. It's entirely under my control. Another person's actions may rile me, but they can't possibly determine response. I'm the only person with the power to do that. And God tells me to be concerned with *my* responses (the choices I make), not my mate's actions.

I'm fully aware that what I just described is far from easy to do. But by God's grace and His provision as we rely on Him, it can be done, albeit imperfectly. You and I can choose to do the right thing.

GET THE DETAILS RIGHT

John Wooden is arguably the best college basketball coach of all time, winning ten national championships in a twelve-year period at UCLA. Before Wooden ever taught a kid one thing about basketball, he'd personally show the player how to put on his socks and lace and tie his shoes "precisely."[10] In defending this meticulousness, Wooden said, "When you see a successful individual, a champion, a 'winner,' you can be very sure that you are looking at an individual who pays great attention to the perfection of minor details."[11] A great marriage and a great sex life result from perfecting minor details.

I've had men say to me, "You're so lucky. I really envy you and Amy. I can see how much you love each other simply by the way you look at each other. But I just don't feel that way about my wife. I've decided to end this marriage so I can be free to find someone I can really be happy with."

I respond by saying, "Yes, we do love each other, but since you've never lived with us, you haven't seen the several kazillion times I've done my The World Revolves Around Me Dance. Neither have you seen lightning bolts flash from my wife's lovely eyes, burning huge holes straight through my retinas, causing my head to explode right there on the spot." Next, I try to tell them that luck really has nothing to do with it. A good marriage is all about trusting God and putting your socks on the right way.

Chalking up a successful marriage to luck is similar to walking into an immaculate house and saying, "You sure are lucky this place is so clean," implying that your hosts were fortunate enough to buy a house that somehow cleans itself. We know that the clean, orderly house with the beautiful flower garden has somebody taking care of it. Likewise, great marriages and great sex lives don't just happen. They are created by faith in God and by consistent, hard work.

That's what it means to take great care with the basics of holy sex. To have a great, God-honoring, soul-touching sexual relationship, we must seek our mate's needs above our own.

We must seek oneness above pleasure. We must seek to destroy whatever pictures of love, sex, bodies, and marriage we have that do not line up with the truth of God's Word. We must ruthlessly battle against any outside force (pornography, abuse, other relationships) that would seek to destroy our intimacy. We must accept our mates just as they are, as God's perfect gift. We must see sex as a celebration of God's presence. We must enter into utmost intimacy with our mates with a perspective of sacredness, holiness, and grace.

Doing these things doesn't take a genius, but it does take careful attention to the details. There are elements of faith, elements of understanding, and elements of acting upon what we know God calls us to do. If you and I want to experience marriage and sexual intimacy in the way that truly brings lasting fulfillment, we must daily choose to love, choose to cherish, and choose to honor. In the Old Testament, the Promised Land was open to all Israelites. Today, the Promised Land of holy, God-honoring, and mutually fulfilling sex is open to all who faithfully seek it. As sex therapist Doug Rosenau has said, "Christians have the ability to be the best lovers in the world."[12] They can be the best lovers because they know the One who invented sex—and the One who will lead them into the land of milk and honey.

THE SEXUAL WILDERNESS

With all this talk of oneness, intimacy, and God-honoring sex, you may be thinking that I don't understand the depth of your pain or the complete lack of intimacy that you feel with your spouse. If you think that, you're right. I don't understand, because I'm not where you are. But God does understand. And His promises are not just for those who currently enjoy warm, caring marriages. God is bigger than any hurt and greater than any cold relationship. He can bring you out of the wilderness and into the Promised Land.

While I was finishing the last few chapters of this book, four couples very close to Amy and me each experienced a marital crisis. Two of these marriages are ending in divorce, while two other couples are fighting to survive. To put it bluntly, this has shaken our world. People we love are suffering the pain of marriages falling apart; they are failing to enter the Promised Land. In addition to our sadness, our prayers, and the continued extension of our friendship, we've been asking ourselves: "Why do people still make bad choices when they've been confronted with the 'right thing to do'?"

I don't have the answer to that question. We can't force people to make different choices. I don't know what will cause you to choose either to walk out of a marriage, to be satisfied with a mediocre marriage, or to enter the Promised Land of a great marriage and an intimate, enriching sex life. But I do know where God wants you, and I do know that He has provided the path for you to get there. He wants you to keep climbing until you reach the summit of holy sex.

But back to the mediocre option. The word *mediocre* comes from two Latin words meaning "halfway" and "stony mountain." So the word literally means to go halfway up the stony mountain—and stop. It implies that when you started your journey, your intentions were to go all the way to the summit, but the pressures and pain of the climb caused you to stop climbing; sooner or later you became satisfied with the view from halfway up. But stopping halfway is nothing like reaching the top. The thrill and joy are not the same; the experience is mediocre. God doesn't want mediocre, and neither do you. God wants us to keep climbing until we reach the top.

If you're struggling with what to do to rekindle love, joy, passion, and intimacy in your marriage, I encourage you to heed the advice that Christ gave to the church at Ephesus: "Do the things you did at first" (Revelation 2:5). Christ is admonishing a group of Christians whose hearts for Him have grown cold. He is encouraging them to do the things they did when they were first in love with Him. The advice applies to marriage as well. When you first fell in love with your mate, it wasn't because you tripped over a box of chocolates. It was because you both were *doing things* that created love.

Next, I challenge you to follow the advice I first heard attributed to a newspaper advice columnist named George Crane. A woman wrote to Crane, saying she wanted to get back at her husband for hurting her. Crane told the woman to treat her husband like a king for thirty days, convincing him how much she loved him, and then suddenly leave him. That, Crane told her, would really hurt. As you have guessed, at the end of thirty days, this woman discovered she really did love her husband.[13]

Love is proactive; it takes initiative; it's something you do. But doing it for just a day or two won't work; love takes time. Doing the deeds of love continually will bring the conviction and the feelings of love—continually.

THE POWER OF VISION

My appointment book has been a conversation starter ever since I got married. It's not the book itself, but rather the photo that I placed on the first page—my wedding picture. I've been known to do some weird things, but this is not one of them. The purpose is simple: to remind myself over and over again of the commitments I made to Amy the day we married. Those commitments included to live together "by God's design in the holy state of matrimony," and they included the belief that (to paraphrase Jeremiah 29:11) God had plans to prosper us and not to harm us, plans to give us a hope and a future together.

God has plans to prosper you as well. Therefore, you should sit down together as husband and wife and develop a shared vision for your marriage. The power of vision can move people and corporations; the power of God's vision can move mountains—and marriages. Someone much wiser than I am once said, "Do not sacrifice the glory of the eternal on the altar of the immediate." That, too, is something I've placed where I can read it every day. It reminds me and challenges me to avoid all behaviors that can threaten the intimacy of my marriage, both in the present and the future. It's a blatant proclamation that there is no selfish pleasure or gratification on the face of this earth that's worth jeopardizing the glory of lifelong marriage, the glory of living in the Promised Land.

So I encourage you, as husband and wife, to fall on your knees and offer your marriage, your sexual intimacy, and your future to God. Put them in His hands. Know that He has plans for you—plans for a hope and a future. You can envision paradise on earth—the Promised Land—and God can take you there.

NOT SAFE, JUST RIGHT

In C. S. Lewis's classic *The Lion, the Witch, and the Wardrobe*, Mr. Beaver is preparing to take the children to meet Aslan, the King. Nervous about the prospect of meeting the Great Lion, Lucy asks if Aslan is safe. "Safe?" Mr. Beaver replies, "Of course he isn't safe. But he's good."[14]

Ultimately marriage isn't safe, but it is good. It isn't safe to know and be fully known by another. It isn't safe to commit to fulfill your mate's desires while putting your own needs on the back burner. It isn't safe to enter into the mystery of holy sexuality where everything is exposed. It's ultimately a risk to walk into the Promised Land and face the giants who reside there. To do these things, you must trust God and your mate. But in reality, people don't want a life that's completely safe. They would rather take the risks involved in being known and being loved. That's how God made us. Letting yourself be known and loved may not be safe, but it's entirely good. As a matter of fact, God calls it marriage, and He calls marriage "very good" (Genesis 1:31).

And God has called you to celebrate this mystery. You must be willing, by His grace, to view His gift of sex as a divine passage into the holy. You must take the high view of Scripture that sexual intimacy has always been intended to represent Christ and His church. You must act on the seriousness of Scripture that says the only valid reason to abstain from marital sexual intimacy for a time is to devote yourselves to prayer (1 Corinthians 7:5). And you must commit to experience the fun and playfulness of sexual joy as it's described in Scripture in the relationship of Solomon and his bride (see the Song of Songs). You don't have to settle for mediocrity. You have choices you can make; you have a covenant to keep. And God gives you the power to do so.

In the covenant of marriage, you and I can experience and celebrate sexual intimacy with our spouses in a way that lasts and that ultimately fulfills. We can know that God smiles down from heaven as we share in the love that He created. We can live and thrive within the mystery and joy of oneness. We can enter into worship as we rejoice in God's presence with us. We can know and be fully known; we can be naked and truly unashamed. We can enter the Promised Land of marriage that God has designed for us.

We can do all of this. Because our God is a God of grace. Because of the cross of Christ.

And because sex is holy.

QUESTIONS FOR CONVERSATION

1. Let's start with a tough assignment. Make a list of three things you can do to make your mate feel more loved and cherished. Include those things you know you've been avoiding. Don't share your list with your spouse. Just go ahead and "do it."

2. Do you agree that marriage is a covenant, not a contract? Why or why not? Discuss how your marriage can be more of a covenant relationship than it has been in the past.

3. Share your memories of your wedding day, particularly the ceremony. What do you remember about your vows? If you have a cassette or videotape of your wedding, get it out and play it. Did either one of you say, "As long as I feel like it"? Repeat your vows to one another. Prayerfully commit to each other to live in the way that God desires husbands and wives to live.

4. Have you perfected the basics of a God-honoring marriage and sexual relationship? Talk with each other about which basics you think you do well and which ones you still need to work on.

5. Are you committed to choosing the right thing at all times? Take time to write a letter to your spouse, and in it pledge to fulfill the basics of a God-honoring marriage. Also in your letter, describe specifically how you will "do the right thing."

6. Do you have a vision for your marriage? If so, share with each other what it is. If not, discuss together what you'd like it to be. Share answers to these questions: What do you want to be doing together ten years from now? Fifteen? Twenty-five? What do you want your marriage to be remembered for? What traits of a God-honoring marriage do you most value? What will each of you do to improve in every one of these areas?

7. Are you ready to enter the Promised Land of sacred sex? If so, commit to praying together, at least four times per week, that God will take you there. Remember that marriage is not safe, but marriage is good. Know, too, that all things good are possible with and through the cross of Christ. Step out, trust God, and go into the land that the Lord, your God, has given you.

Notes

Chapter 1

1. For more on this idea, see Shmuley Boteach, *Kosher Sex: A Recipe for Passion and Intimacy* (New York: Doubleday, 1999), 46.

2. R. C. Sproul, *The Holiness of God* videotape series (Muskegon, Mich.: Gospel Films, 1998), vol. 1.

3. Walter Trobisch, *I Loved a Girl* (New York: Harper & Row, 1965).

4. Patricia DiLucchio, "Know When to Say When" (online women's advice column); http://www.women.com, accessed September 13, 1999, http://womenswire.com/sexpert/do923sex.2html.

5. Eric Schlosser, "The Business of Pornography," *U.S. News & World Report,* 10 February 1997.

6. Victor Strasburger, "Adolescent Medicine," *State of the Art Reviews,* vol. 4, no. 3 (Philadelphia, Pa.: Hanley & Belfus, October 1993).

7. David Reuben, *Everything You Always Wanted to Know About Sex But Were Afraid to Ask* (New York: Bantam, 1971). This concept runs throughout Reuben's book.

8. R. C. Sproul, *The Intimate Marriage* (Wheaton, Ill.: Tyndale, 1986), 90.

9. Stephen Sapp, *Sexuality, the Bible, and Science* (Philadelphia, Pa.: Fortress, 1977), 18.

10. Bill Hybels and Rob Wilkins, *Tender Love* (Chicago: Moody, 1993), 14.

11. Saint Augustine, *The Confessions* (London: Penguin, 1961), 132.

12. Boteach, *Kosher Sex,* 10.

13. Hybels and Wilkins, *Tender Love,* 14.

14. From a talk given by Jerry Wunder at a FamilyLife Marriage Conference. © 1994 Campus Crusade for Christ International.

15. Sapp, *Sexuality, the Bible, and Science,* 7.

16. M. Scott Peck, *Further Along the Road Less Traveled* (New York: Touchstone/Simon & Schuster, 1993), 220.

17. Boteach, *Kosher Sex,* 46.

18. Boteach, *Kosher Sex,* 55.

Chapter 2

1. For purposes of illustration, I've created composite couples whose experiences mirror the struggles of many clients I have counseled. By combining their experiences, I can protect their confidentiality as well as demonstrate a comforting truth: You and I are not alone in the struggles, confusion, frustration, or pain surrounding our sexuality.

2. A. Skevington Wood, *Ephesians, The Expositor's Bible Commentary,* Frank Gaebelein, general editor (Grand Rapids, Mich.: Zondervan, 1978), 2:75.

3. Wood, *Ephesians,* 2:77.

4. John Sailhamer, *Genesis Unbound: A Provocative New Look at the Creation Account* (Sisters, Oreg.: Multnomah, 1996), 24.

5. Richard M. Davidson, *The Theology of Sexuality in the Beginning,* vol. 26, no. 1 (Andrews University Seminary Studies, Summer 1988), 6.

6. Davidson, *The Theology of Sexuality in the Beginning,* 8.

7. Walter Brueggemann, *Genesis: An Interpretation* (Atlanta, Ga.: John Knox, 1982), 47.

8. Stephen Sapp, *Sexuality, the Bible, and Science* (Philadelphia, Pa.: Fortress, 1977), 10.

Chapter 3

1. Shmuley Boteach, *Kosher Sex: A Recipe for Passion and Intimacy* (New York: Doubleday, 1999), 28.

2. W. E. Vine, Merrill F. Unger, and William White Jr., *Vine's Complete Expository Dictionary of Old and New Testament Words* (Nashville, Tenn.: Thomas Nelson, 1996), 130.

3. Boteach, *Kosher Sex,* 37.

4. Howard Marshall, A. R. Millard, J. I. Packer, and D. J. Wiseman, eds., *New Bible Dictionary,* 3d ed. (Leicester, England: InterVarsity, 1996), 1250.

5. *New Bible Dictionary,* 1250.

6. "Worship," *Holman Bible Dictionary,* © 1991 Holman Bible Publishers. Used by special arrangement with Broadman & Holman, Nashville, Tenn. Database © 1997 NavPress Software, program WORDSearch.

7. "Worship," *Holman Bible Dictionary,* 1997.

8. See Acts 7:48.

9. Mircea Eliade, *The Sacred and the Profane: The Nature of Religion* (New York: Harvest/Harcourt Brace Jovanovich, 1959), 14.

10. Boteach, *Kosher Sex,* 46.

11. Stephen Sapp, *Sexuality, the Bible, and Science* (Philadelphia, Pa.: Fortress, 1977), 28.

12. John Ortberg, *The Life You've Always Wanted* (Grand Rapids, Mich.: Zondervan, 1997), 72.

13. Scott Stanley et al., *A Lasting Promise* (San Francisco: Jossey-Bass, 1998), 263.

Chapter 4

1. Scott Stanley et al., *A Lasting Promise* (San Francisco: Jossey-Bass, 1998), 263.

2. Dan Allender, *The Wounded Heart* (Colorado Springs, Colo.: Nav-Press, 1993), 49.

3. Let me offer an essential caveat to this discussion of the complete acceptance of one's mate. Acceptance does not mean we put up with harmful, destructive behavior. God does not want us to tolerate abuse, a sexual affair, a partner's addiction to pornography, alcohol, or drugs, or any other destructive behavior. Those situations must be dealt with head-on and without retreat or compromise.

4. Larry Crabb, *The Marriage Builder* (Grand Rapids, Mich.: Zondervan, 1982), 20.

5. Crabb, *The Marriage Builder,* 35.

6. Crabb, *The Marriage Builder,* 34.

7. C. S. Lewis, *The Four Loves* (San Diego, Calif.: Harcourt Brace, 1960), 106.

Chapter 5

1. Linda Dillow and Lorraine Pintus, *Intimate Issues: Conversations Woman to Woman* (Colorado Springs, Colo.: WaterBrook, 1999), 180.

2. Scott Stanley et al., *A Lasting Promise* (San Francisco: Jossey-Bass, 1998), 254.

3. John Trent, *Love for All Seasons* (Chicago: Moody, 1996), 113.

4. Dillow and Pintus, *Intimate Issues,* 222.

5. Dillow and Pintus, *Intimate Issues,* 222.

6. Dillow and Pintus, *Intimate Issues,* 224.

7. Dillow and Pintus, *Intimate Issues,* 223.

8. John Ortberg, *The Life You've Always Wanted* (Grand Rapids, Mich.: Zondervan, 1997), 59.

Chapter 6

1. Lewis Smedes, *Sex for Christians* (Grand Rapids, Mich.: Eerdmans, 1976), 29.
2. Colin Brown, ed., *The New International Dictionary of New Testament Theology* (Grand Rapids, Mich.: Zondervan, 1971), 1056.
3. Archibald Hart, Catherine Hart Weber, and Debra Taylor, *The Secrets of Eve* (Nashville, Tenn.: Word, 1998), 72.
4. For a detailed study of this topic, see Gary Chapman, *The Five Love Languages* (Chicago: Northfield, 1992).
5. C. S. Lewis, *The Four Loves* (San Diego, Calif.: Harcourt Brace, 1960), 99.
6. Linda Dillow and Lorraine Pintus, *Intimate Issues: Conversations Woman to Woman* (Colorado Springs, Colo.: WaterBrook, 1999).

Chapter 7

1. Mars Hill Audio, *Uncharted Waters: Dockside Gambling in Tunnica, Mississippi* (Charlottesville, Va.: Berea, 2000). For more information, visit http://www.marshillaudio.org.
2. John Gray, *Mars and Venus in the Bedroom* (New York: Harper-Perennial, 1995), 23.
3. R. C. Sproul, *The Intimate Marriage* (Wheaton, Ill.: Tyndale, 1975), 105-6.
4. Sproul, *The Intimate Marriage*, 104.
5. Everett Worthington Jr., *Trainer's Manual for Hope-Focused Marital Enrichment* (Richmond: Virginia Commonwealth University Press), 76. Document published for research use only. © Everett Worthington Jr.

6. For more information, read Robert T. Michael et al., *Sex in America: A Definitive Survey* (Boston: Little, Brown, 1994).

7. Gary Smalley, *Love Is a Decision* (Nashville, Tenn.: Word, 1989), 178.

8. You can contact FamilyLife Today at http://www.familylife.com. Or call toll-free 1-800-FLTODAY.

Chapter 8

1. Gary Brooks, *The Centerfold Syndrome* (San Francisco: Jossey-Bass, 1995), 100.

2. C. S. Lewis, *The Four Loves* (San Diego, Calif.: Harcourt Brace, 1960), 101.

3. Lewis, *The Four Loves*, 101.

4. Janin Friend, "In Depth: Executive Health & Fitness," *American Business Journal* (Web version: 28 June 1999; print edition: 25 June 1999).

5. Notes from Julie Hayes, R.D., University of California, Santa Barbara, curriculum on the film *Still Killing Us Softly*, 1992.

6. Figures released by the U.S. Bureau of Consumer Protection of the Federal Trade Commission, Report on the Public Conference on Commercial Weight Loss Products and Programs, 16-17 October 1997.

7. Report on the Public Conference on Commercial Weight Loss Products and Programs.

8. Notes from Julie Hayes.

9. Statistics from American City Business Journals, Inc., Jim Meyers, 8 January 1999 print edition; http://www.bizjournals.com.

10. *Fortune Small Business* report, 28 November 2000; http://www.fsb.com, FSB 25.

11. U.S. Food and Drug Administration, *FDA Consumer Magazine,* "Hair Replacement: What Works, What Doesn't," Larry Hanover, April 1977, http://www.fda.gov.

12. Hoover's Online, *The Business Network,* http://www.hoovers.com.

13. Tatiana D. Helenius, "Romance Novels, The Facts," *CNN Financial Network,* 23 August 2000.

14. Richard Foster, *Celebration of Discipline,* rev. ed. (San Francisco: HarperSanFrancisco, 1988), 80.

15. Marilyn Yalom, *A History of the Breast* (New York: Random House, 1997), 59.

16. Notes from Julie Hayes.

17. Yalom, *A History of the Breast,* 3.

18. Brooks, *The Centerfold Syndrome,* 3.

19. Notes from Julie Hayes.

20. Brooks, *The Centerfold Syndrome,* 4.

21. Michael Ausiello, "The Skinny on Courtney Thorne-Smith," *TV Guide Online, Insider,* 5 December 2000.

Chapter 9

1. Haddon W. Robinson, message delivered at Denver Seminary chapel service, Denver, Colorado, 1983.

2. Anonymous, "The War Within: An Anatomy of Lust," *Leadership Journal,* vol. 3, no. 4, Fall 1982, 33.

Chapter 10

1. Gordon P. Hugenberger, *Marriage As a Covenant* (Grand Rapids, Mich.: Baker, 1994), 171.

2. Hugenberger, *Marriage As a Covenant,* 180.

3. Hugenberger, *Marriage As a Covenant,* 216.

4. Hugenberger, *Marriage As a Covenant,* 201.

5. Hugenberger, *Marriage As a Covenant,* 230.

6. Scott Stanley, *The Heart of Commitment* (Nashville, Tenn.: Thomas Nelson, 1998), 1-2. I highly recommend this book for an in-depth discussion of marital commitment.

7. Ken Gire, *Intimate Moments with the Savior* (Grand Rapids, Mich.: Zondervan, 1989), 24.

8. M. Craig Barnes, *Yearning* (Downer's Grove, Ill.: InterVarsity, 1991), 20. Special thanks to Pastor Dave Rodriquez for linking together the insights of Ken Gire and M. Craig Barnes.

9. Stanley, *The Heart of Commitment,* 20.

10. John R. Wooden, *Wooden: A Lifetime of Observations and Reflections On and Off the Court* (New York: McGraw-Hill, 1997), 61.

11. Wooden, *Wooden,* 63.

12. Doug Rosenau, *A Celebration of Sex* (Nashville, Tenn.: Thomas Nelson, 1994), 10.

13. I have heard several versions of this story, though initially from Dr. Vernon Grounds, chancellor of Denver Seminary. A most worthy source, I must say.

14. C. S. Lewis, *The Lion, the Witch, and the Wardrobe* (New York: HarperCollins, 1950), 86.

Acknowledgments

Of all the creatures of God who grace this planet, I first and foremost want to thank my lovely wife, Amy. You have faithfully loved me in every sense of the word through three children, four moves, two careers, two graduate programs, numerous articles, good times, tough times (there have been no bad times), and now a book. Though I've written a whole book, I could never find the right words to tell you what you mean to me. Thank you for believing in me, for loving me, for being you. May there forever be days on the beach.

To my children, Austin, Caleb, and Gracie, for giving me an occasional break from wrestling on the floor, sparring in tae kwon do, getting donuts, reading books, and playing games and every kind of sport long enough to write a book and a dissertation (and for letting me use the computer). I have learned so much about what God must feel as a Father by having you in my life. Your support means all the world to me. You're my favorite fan club and it was a blast celebrating the book in style with you in Colorado.

To the great people at WaterBrook Press: Laura Wright, Kirsten Blomquist, Michele Tennesen, and especially my editor, Ron Lee. Ron, you believed in me as an unknown magazine writer and have now believed in me as an unknown book writer. You were always willing to say, "Good stuff," at one paragraph and two lines later say, "Maybe it's me, but you really lost me here." Thanks for your encouragement, your friendship, and your hospitality. This is a much better book because of you. As the sign says, "Lee, keeps hanging in there."

I want to thank Tim and Barbara Gardner, my mom and dad: my mom for instilling in me a love for books and knowledge; my dad for always encouraging me to go my own way and making me comfortable with who I was—including losing my hair. For both for teaching me that hard work and sacrifice pay off.

To the friends and family who have read and offered feedback, especially Buddy and Debbie Dunn. Deb, your comments and insights were more valuable than you know; they have made this a better tool for ministry. Thanks for the coffee time in Destin and the stories! I am blessed with great friends.

Thanks to the friends and professionals in the field who have encouraged me in this project: Dr. Doug Rosenau, Dr. Gary Oliver, and especially Dr. Scott Stanley. Scott stood with me at an American Association of Christian Counselors world conference as we discussed these ideas and said, "You can look around here but you won't find another book like this around; if you don't write it, I'm going to." Not only did Scott spur me on to write, but he also read first drafts and offered great insight and much needed critique. Thank you for all your help.

To my doctoral study group, the management team of The Cabin Counseling Center, and all my friends at Zionsville Presbyterian Church. As my church family, you have given much, endured much, loved much, prayed much—and you have taught me much. To my partner, Deidra, for constant encouragement; to Nancy for annotations, support, and laughing at my jokes; to Glenn for all of your wisdom and insight and the rest of the staff and leadership of ZPC for always letting me go the way I felt God calling. I am blessed. Thanks for the sabbatical!

To all my counseling clients who have shared their hearts and their hurts with me. You have taught me much; you have made me grow. I am indebted:

To the faculty of The School of Theology at Anderson University, and especially to Dr. Juanita Leonard.

To Dr. Vernon Grounds at Denver Seminary for first fanning into flame the desire to write and for teaching me that theology and psychology are not necessarily polar opposites.

To Stan and Debbie for always being there as an example of God's ways and a constant support in times of trouble.

To Kurt and Vicky for your friendship and a great place to write.

And a special thanks to all the people who have faithfully prayed for me; those I know and those I don't.

Okay, I'd like to thank Amy one more time for not only encouraging me to write this book—but also for teaching me and living out its truth. Thanks for your love and your constant acceptance of my goofiness—because to write a book on sex and then have to sleep on the couch would be a real bummer.

And finally and forever—to the sovereign God of the universe who sent His Son and my Savior, Jesus Christ, so that we could know Him. You have opened the storehouses of heaven as You have blessed me with a call, a conviction, life, children, and an amazing wife. Any truth found within this book is from Him and Him alone; any failure or faulty teaching is mine and mine alone. This book is only as good as it is measured by bringing people closer to Him.

If you would like to contact Tim Gardner, please write to him at one of the following addresses:

Tim@marriageinstitute.org

http://www.marriageinstitute.org

Tim Gardner
The Marriage Institute
P.O. Box 602
Westfield, IN 46074

To learn more about WaterBrook Press and view
our catalog of products, log on to our Web site:
www.waterbrookpress.com

WATER BROOK
PRESS